LOVE

To live, you must love more

&

ENTROPY

ROBERT L. FAY, JR

Love & Entropy

Copyright © 2025 Robert L. Fay, Jr

ISBN (Paperback): 979-8-89672-234-2
ISBN (Ebook): 979-8-89672-235-9

Printed in the United States of America.

PROMINENT
BOOKS
EDGE

5830 E 2nd St, Ste 7000 #9983
Casper, WY 82609
USA

CONTENTS

Dedicated to my Mom and Dad
who were my first and best teachers of how to
love God, myself and my neighbors.

INTRODUCTION

I was a good, practicing Catholic for the first 24 years of my life. A churchgoer every Sunday that made all the sacraments (Baptism, Reconciliation, First Communion, Confirmation and Holy Matrimony) and thought this part of my life was under control. Then my former college roommate invited me and my new wife of three months over for dinner.

After showing us around the brand-new log cabin-style house that he built from a kit, we sat to eat. He said that he wanted to begin with a blessing and took a deep cleansing breath then launched into a fire and brimstone type prayer. I sheepishly looked up to see who had taken possession of my old friend. As soon as the blessing was over, he quickly jumped into what seemed to be a prepared speech about how he and his wife were "saved", and he couldn't wait to tell us about it and help us become "saved" as well. He then proceeded to attack everything I believed in as a Roman Catholic and why my church (which used to be his church) was evil and, thank God he and his family are now "born again". He completely believed that his fundamentalist, non-denominational church approach was the way to go if we had any hope of making it to Heaven. As an Irish Catholic, with two uncles, a Jesuit Priest and a Deacon, an aunt who was in a convent and many, many practicing Catholic relatives, I was not going to take this attack of our faith. I objected to what he was saying with the good Catholic propaganda I learned over the years. My answers lacked real substance and I couldn't come up with meaningful reasons why I believed anything I just said. We fought for hours while our wives quietly looked on. It was clear that I was beaten badly and lost this battle (not the war, just this battle).

I didn't realize it at the time, but he did "save" me that night from a mediocre spiritual life of going through the motions. It woke me up and made me realize that I was sleep walking with no real understanding of what my "religion" was all about. Think about it, most of us understand as much as a twelve-year-old when it comes to our religion[1]. We dutifully went to classes as children, met all the minimum standards but didn't think too much about it. At that point, about age twelve, we thought we graduated from religious study never to return to it. Many go through their whole life without thinking too hard again about their religious beliefs. Until recently you'd never see a religious book (besides the Bible) on the New York Times best seller list. That seems to be changing as more and more people start asking what that great bumper sticker said, "What if the Hokey-Pokey is all its about?"

Dinner and our argument ended so we thanked our hosts and ran for the exit as fast as we could. My wife couldn't stop talking about how our friends had gone over the edge, but I secretly pledged to myself that I would find the answers to reengage him in battle one day. This vow is still very much a part of me as I am writing this book forty six years later still trying to effectively respond to his arguments. I have learned some valuable things along the way that, I hope, will be helpful to anyone else that gets sandbagged like that by a friend.

> 1. U.S. Conference of Catholic Bishops said that in the U.S., the age of celebrating confirmation is between the age of reason (around 7) and age 16.

I began my search for better answers by reading up on solid Catholic sources. I took a Knights of Columbus home study course, read several books; listened to tapes, read Catholic tracks and anything I could get my hands on to respond to my friend. With, what I thought was great ammunition, I fired up a long, well documented letter. He quickly responded with a small booklet that condemned the Catholic Church for all its errors. I picked this booklet apart in detail documenting every answer with the proper footnotes and proudly sent a twenty-page retort believing that I had skillfully handled his objections. Within days I got another booklet that took even more vicious shots at all my beliefs and how the Catholic Church had been "power hungry" and "corrupt" through the ages.

This argument was taking its toll on me. Was everything I learned about God wrong? I went to see my local Pastor and asked for help. He told me that there was a "Cursillo" weekend being held at a local retreat house in a week and he thought I should go. Cursillo was a church movement started to teach adult Catholics more about their faith. It literally meant "A Little Course in Christianity". He thought it would be difficult to get me in on such late notice, but he would try. Later that day he called amazed that someone had dropped out at the last minute and there was one available opening. I decided that God wanted me there and went expecting to be enlightened and armed with all kinds of new bombs to hurl at my misguided friend.

The weekend began with a welcoming reception on Thursday night. Expecting to run into a whole bunch of "holier than me" Catholic know it all's, I was pleasantly surprised by how "normal" and friendly the participants and the leaders seemed. Classes started early the next day and the schedule was packed with informative but not earth-shattering insights. By Saturday night I was disappointed that God didn't seem to be speaking directly to me. I wasn't expecting a private audience or a voice from the heavens, but I did feel that something important would happen during the weekend and I was not feeling it. Then it happened. The leader of the course asked each of us to make a chapel visit alone sometime Saturday night. He said we should go there with a specific question in mind and we would receive our answer. That was Saturday night, October 13, 1979, the night that changed my life forever.

The leader said spend time in your rooms thinking hard about what you want to ask and when you are ready go to the chapel. I didn't need time to think about it, my question is the one I came to the retreat with. Walking slowly into a dimly lit chapel, I knelt before the Tabernacle to ask my question, "Are you real and why are we here?" As my knees hit the carpet, I felt a firm hand on my back, pushing me to the floor. The room lit up and I was staring at the bare feet of a person in a long white robe. I stood up but realized my body was still on the floor and told myself, I am not my body. I felt wide awake, not like this was a dream, but an unbelievable experience.

He put his hands on my shoulders. I stared at him, but his face was shielded by a cloud. I could only make out his bearded mouth and chin. He was slightly taller than me, about 6 feet or so. He leaned in and started talking but I heard nothing. It was like listening to the television news with the volume turned down. It seemed like he was saying something extremely important, but I couldn't hear a thing. I thought that he must want to tell my spirit something that I didn't need to hear. I really wanted him to speak up but wouldn't dare interrupt.

As I surveyed my surroundings, there was an armored angel behind the man that appeared to be guarding a door. I sensed another angel behind me but never turned around to verify. The person in front of me stopped moving his mouth and smiled like a proud parent. I wasn't at all afraid; I felt welcomed, loved and peaceful. The next thing I knew, I was back on the floor alone in the dark. I jumped up, feeling embarrassed, and quickly looked around hoping nobody was watching me make a fool of myself. Then I raced out of the chapel and for several years, never said a word to anyone about the whole episode.

This happened forty six years ago, but it seems like it was yesterday. I have spent the rest of my life trying to figure out what it all meant and what my spirit knows that I don't. I learned one thing, we are not our human bodies, we are spiritual beings temporarily using our bodies as a vehicle on our journey home. When I was standing outside my body, I was thinking without using the brain that remained on the floor. So, I concluded, that our souls must think independently of our physical bodies. That is why you hear about people floating above their bodies in a hospital and knowing what is happening in the operating room and in other places. The soul must be thinking for itself, not using the unconscious brain in the body on the operating table.

I believe the one pushing me to the floor was my guardian angel. I didn't know it at the time but prostrating oneself on the floor is part of many religious rituals. It is a sign of humility and respect for the one you are meeting. Major world religions employ prostration as an act of submissiveness or worship to a supreme being. I believe that the bearded man in the vision was Jesus and the angel behind him in armor was Michael the Arch Angel. Michael is known as the protector and the leader of the army of God against the forces of evil. I always thought evil was the opposite of love. "Evil" spelled backwards is "live" (I digress). Anyway, he was standing outside a large door that I assumed was the entrance to Heaven. I might be completely wrong, but that is how I interpreted what I saw. None of these symbols, however, helped me figure out what Jesus told my soul that day.

I read up on near-death experiences. Many times, a religious figure, like Jesus, would appear to the near-death person and tell them something important that they would hear and understand.[3] Why was my experience one where the "religious figure" moved his mouth but said nothing out loud? I really wished I heard the message. It was as if he was speaking to my soul and I was just a spectator. Why his face was fogged over by a cloud? Later, I learned that many religions say that we are not allowed to see the face of God until we die. My experience felt like I died, but I didn't. So then, under the circumstances, it probably was a good thing that I didn't see his whole face.

From the moment of my vision until now, I have lost all fear of dying. I am convinced that there is a much larger life beyond the eighty or so years we exist as humans on Earth. I think the scene I saw playing out was the judgment scene we will all experience when we die. Jesus will speak to our soul and know right away if we are prepared to enter Heaven. The Bible depicts a big judgment scene with Jesus separating the wheat from the chaff, but I envision this more personal judgment scene as each of us die. But what about the Judgment Day described in the Bible? Time is an element of the created universe, not of eternity (this will be explained later). No time, as we know it passes in Heaven. We may not see a relative that died for fifty years, but for them it would be as if no time passed before we are reunited. They are beyond happy in Heaven while we struggle here on earth. That is why I never feel sorry for the person who dies only for those he or she loved that have been left behind. We spend years longing to be with them while they are reunited with us in Heaven in a blink of their eye. So "Judgment Day" is the "minute" we die. It appears to be a different "time" to us but not to God. No time, as we know it, has passed from the time that the first man and woman was created until the last one dies, and the universe is extinguished.

On the final day of the Cursillo, the instructor spent a significant amount of time talking about the Creator and how the universe was made "In His Image". As a frustrated artist that never pursued my love of drawing and painting, the idea of the Creator being an artist and the creation being his artwork made sense to me. If you study a work of art, you can learn a lot about the person who created it. So, this is where my journey began: learning more about Him by studying His "artwork".

I drove home thinking this experience was extremely powerful and life changing. I didn't realize, at the time, that it was the beginning of a life-long search for humanity's purpose. I learn something new every day about "Why we are here".

3. "Near Death Experiences" by P.M.H. Atwater, page 22.

CHAPTER ONE

Why Are We Here?

"To my mind there must be, at the bottom of it all, not an equation, but an utterly simple idea, and to me that idea, when we finally discover it will be so compelling, so inevitable that we will say to one another, 'Oh, how beautiful. How could it be otherwise.'"

—John Archibald Wheeler

What if there is a simple explanation for why we are here, now, in this place? Suppose everything you see was created to help you make a decision that will affect the rest of your life? It is the only decision that matters, and it is a life or death decision. I have spent most of my lifetime investigating it and want to share my results with you.

Let's begin at the beginning. With the help of Edwin Hubble's telescope, scientists have run the movie of time backwards to the birth of the universe some 13.7 billion years ago. They can look back to a fraction of a second after it all started but can't quite see the official starting point. They tell us that before time began, there was absolutely nothing: no matter, energy, fields, structures, properties, potentialities, black holes, dark energy or even the "vacuum". The "vacuum" is *not* nothing; it is a place where bits of matter and antimatter pop up and disappear regularly. So, how did the universe

1

appear out of nowhere? How and why did the universe just pop into existence?

When they play the movie backwards, out of nowhere, a tiny piece of matter suddenly appears. It is about the size of a golf ball but weighs trillions of pounds and its temperature is trillions of degrees. As they begin to play the movie forward, the ball increases to about the size of a grapefruit and then explodes with a big bang, spewing its contents in all directions. They tell us that little ball contained all the energy and matter that there would ever be. Then, mysteriously as the universal temperature cooled, the pieces began uniting forming galaxies, stars, solar systems, planets, moons, and finally life on earth. The newly formed life wasn't much to speak of for millions of years, just single celled bacteria. But something changed; the single celled organisms began joining together to form multi-celled organisms. Over time, somehow, those miniature organisms multiplied into trillion-celled human organisms. Amazing. Was it all random or part of a divine plan?

If it was not designed exactly as it was, human life would not be possible here on earth. That's right, if things didn't happen exactly as they did, we would not be here.

> "The laws of nature seem to have been crafted to move the universe toward the emergence and sustenance of life."
> —Physicist Freeman Dyson

I wondered, what was the force that created that initial universal seed? How could it possibly contain all the energy and the plans for all the matter that there would ever be for as long as this universe existed? I didn't realize it at the time, but this early "birth of the universe" story contained all we need to know to understand why we are here and what we must do to continue to live.

Science teaches us that everything in the universe has a reason to exist or it vanishes. Approximately 99.9 percent of all things that have emerged in the universe have already disappeared. So why do we think humanity is so special and why are we *still here*?

You probably have read about people who have near-death experiences and then claim they have become enlightened and think they have all the answers to life's big questions. They really don't have all the answers and don't even know all the questions. Even if they witnessed the magnificence of God or Heaven, they still can only rely on their limited consciousness to interpret what they saw. Some claim they can tap into the cosmic mind of the universe and find whatever answers they need but the universe is a creation of God, just like us, that had a beginning and will end. Even if people could commune with the universal mind, it was created in time and would be limited in what it could comprehend based on its own "consciousness". The universe is infinitesimal compared to God or eternity. So, we need to be careful about drawing too many conclusions from it. Making the universe god, is putting a false god ahead of the real one and only God.

Science

I didn't like science in high school and vowed to never take a science class in college and never did. But after my "experience", I felt drawn to science books. I say "experience" because I'm not sure how "near death" I was at the time and my doctor never detected any signs of a physical problem that could have caused a "near death" experience. But when people describe their near-death experiences, it sure sounds like what happened to me. After my vision, I found myself going to book stores and wandering around. A small voice in my head would point me to a book and, without thinking too hard about it, I would buy it.

At first, I thought I was just selecting interesting looking books but several books into my research I realized that I was not the one doing the choosing. I would buy books about science, mathematics, health, religion, philosophy, Greek mythology and many other topics I never was that interested in before. Each book had information that became a piece of a larger puzzle I was putting together. I believe that the Holy Spirit was directing me to books that would explain some aspect of God and his purpose. If this was the Holy Spirit's way of illuminating what the man in my vision was telling my spirit, I was willing to play along. Rather than bore you with all the intermediate steps I went through reaching the following conclusion, let's just jump to the bottom line: there seems to be only two primal forces operating in the universe, love and entropy. All other forces are subsets of these two.

Love is the force that holds all things together. It is the binding force, creating bonds, uniting individual parts into greater wholes. It affects all things from sub-atomic particles to human marriage to life itself. Whenever you see two things being joined into one greater whole, you are witnessing universal love at work.

Entropy is the opposite of love. It is the force that tears things apart, breaks bonds, causes thing to disintegrate, grow old and die. Entropy is the natural order of things. It has been around since the beginning of time and will be here until the end. It is the keeper of time. It is the reason why you know what happened yesterday but not tomorrow. Energy begins in a concentrated, condensed space and then, over time, as it cools it spreads out and dissipates as heat. This is the natural flow of all things in our universe.

Entropy is the "nickname" for the Second Law of Thermodynamics. Physics teaches that there are three laws of thermodynamics. The first law states that all the energy that exists in the universe has been here since the beginning and will be here until it is ends. This is because the universe is a closed system that *physically* doesn't allow anything in or out. No energy will ever be added or subtracted. The second law says that energy, in a closed system, will spread out or disperse over time and it will naturally move from potential energy to working or kinetic energy to spent energy or heat. Over time, all the energy in the universe will be converted to heat and the universe will die of heat death. The third law states that the lowest temperature for energy is absolute zero. When all the energy in the universe is converted to heat through entropy, the universal temperature will drop to absolute zero (no more heat) and the universe will be cold, stone dead.

As I learned about entropy it reminded me of sin and evil. Sin means to "miss the mark" or to not do what God wants us to do and, if we don't, we sin. You don't really mean it when you say, "My car is rusty, what a sin". Your car is rusty from entropy, but it isn't a sin. Evil can be initiated by us or happen to us. It is the absence of goodness like darkness is the absence of light. Entropy is a much broader concept than evil or sin. They are a part of entropy but there are other things that entropy does like breaking things apart, separating, destroying, disintegrating and killing. Entropy is a more inclusive description than sin or evil in describing the real forces that oppose God.

Entropy is the natural order of things. It is the natural ruler of the universe and the "original sin" we all carry. The word *devil* comes from the Greek word, *diabollein*, meaning to tear apart, or to divide. The devil is entropy, the ruler of this universe, who must be overthrown.

Life fights the forces of entropy with love uniting cells and forming objects and organisms that can resist its power. Love binds the cells together and continually nourishes them. A human body is made up of a collection of tissues. Each tissue is really a united community of cells, working to accomplish some directed task. On all levels of existence, it is "love" that bonds, binds, connects and brings two things together as one. It is the primal force that opposes entropy. It also is the "supernatural" force that God injected into the universe from the very beginning to save our lives and allow us to choose the path that leads us to Him. It is the Holy Spirit of God's love.

Love and entropy are two little words with big meanings. In this analysis, think of love as the force that binds things together and entropy as the force that tears things apart. So, it is love, that binds hydrogen and oxygen together to create water and it is entropy that causes a house to burn down and disintegrate in a fire.

Just as computer software can be boiled down to zeros and ones, the universe can be boiled down to love and entropy. You can accomplish great things on a computer by manipulating the zeros and ones and you can achieve great things by recognizing and properly using love and entropy. Love and entropy have positive and negative sides. When a man and a woman get together to create a baby, they are using love positively while loving money above all else is using it negatively. Paint flaking off your house is using entropy negatively while breaking down the nutrients in the food you eat is using it positively. The next two chapters will define love and entropy in greater detail and help you recognize them when you see them. Then you can determine if they are being used positively or negatively and what you can do to make them work as they were intended; to improve your life and help you emerge in Heaven.

In the Beginning

> *"God said, 'Let there be light,' and there was light. God saw that the light was good, God divided light from darkness..."*
> —*Genesis 1:3*

Does the Bible begin by comparing the two primal forces: light (love) and darkness (entropy) and call their interaction good? Was the light the "Big Bang" that began the whole thing? How could this gigantic universe have been packed into a tiny golf ball? How does a giant redwood tree grow from a tiny seed? How does a human being with its trillions of cells grow from the mating of just two microscopic cells? The answer is *emergence*. Emergence means creating something new and different from nothing but the components on a lower level. Those components do not have all the qualities of the emergent entity until they unite and create something new and unique. Consider life: it begins as sub-atomic particles which combine to form atoms, then atoms form molecules that unite forming proteins. Proteins establish complex structures that become systems and the systems link together creating organisms like us. Something new emerges at each level of existence that was not present on the lower level. This process is constantly happening throughout the universe. Teilhard de Chardin referred to it as "cosmogenesis", the continuous state of creation. Things constantly changing, growing and, evolving over time.

Emergence is nature's way of creating ever more complex outcomes. Like two lovers, who marry and form a higher union, able to do more together than they could do apart. Or hydrogen and oxygen combining to form water. Water is at a higher level of organization than hydrogen and oxygen and has new properties that were not present at the lower level. It has a new and different energy pattern. There would be no life if water didn't exist. Like a caterpillar becoming a butterfly, it has been transformed into a new form of the same being.

This process of emergence happens throughout nature. Sudden, fully equipped, new levels of biological organization with no intermediate stages just appear. Like sub-atomic ingredients combining to form atoms of non-living things or the cells, tissues, organs and systems emerging to form living beings. The two components, known as agents, interact and something novel emerges. It has become transformed into a new thing or living being. The new whole is very different and much more than the sum of its parts.

Emergence is like the Bible passage when Jesus says, "For when two or three are gathered together in my name, there I am in their midst." (Matt. 18:20). The passage refers to Jesus being with those who gather to pray but it parallels the concept of emergence. When two or more come together in love, they create a powerful union on a higher level and can do much more than either could do alone. That is why there is tremendous power in group prayer.

A married couple merges to help create a child. As the baby grows in its mother's womb, consciousness and awareness emerges. More importantly, a unique, one-of-a-kind soul, emerges with the free will to love. The soul emerges at a specific time and place, from specific DNA and a unique pattern of energy and matter. How can that same soul regenerate in another body through reincarnation? All the variables that went into the creation of that soul would be different. I believe that we have one time to live in this universe, one time to decide to love and one time to die.

Every time we discuss "combining" something on a lower level to create something on a higher level, we are taking about love emerging. It is love at work that builds up all we see in the universe and especially us. We are the product of love emerging on higher and higher levels. Not only that, we exist on three emergent levels:

physical, mental and spiritual. Our physical properties combine to form our mental processes, and both combine to support our spiritual being. Based on my research, I believe that we are here because of love and so is the earth, the solar system, the sun, the galaxies and the whole universe. Where would this love come from? I believe that it came from God, the source of all love.

Universe Created to Choose Love

The late Stephen Hawkins, author of the book "A Brief History of Time", was considered by many to be the most intelligent physicist since Albert Einstein. A man that was so intelligent that he wasn't sure if God existed but couldn't imagine how the universe could have begun without Him. He wrote:

> *"The earth is a medium size planet, orbiting around an average size sun, on the outer suburbs of an ordinary Spiro galaxy itself one of about a million, million galaxies in the observable universe. It does not seem like it is necessary to have so many galaxies or for the universe to appear so uniform in every direction from where we sit. It would be difficult to explain why the universe would have begun as hypothesized by the hot bang theory except by a Creator who intended to create beings like us. The entire universe is held in a delicate balance and the conditions that exist today are the exact conditions that need to exist to support organic life on this planet."*

Isn't it amazing that organic life on planet earth would not be possible unless ingredients from all over the universe converged on earth to make it possible? Hawkins understood this and yet couldn't bring himself to say outright that there must be a creator that orchestrated the whole thing. He had to die to learn the truth about God.

Hopefully we can have enough faith to accept the truth while we are still alive and can act upon it.

I learned that, according to the Anthropic Principle, human beings would not be here unless several cosmic constants were exactly as they are. If they were one part per million-millionth off we would have a totally different universe with no matter, galaxies, stars, planets or us (gulp). Gravity, the speed of light, the weak and strong forces of the universe had to be exactly as they are, for humanity to be here. If the chemicals like helium, hydrogen, oxygen and carbon didn't form, humans wouldn't either. But they weren't present at the beginning of the universe, so they had to emerge later somehow. For instance, there was no water, an essential ingredient for life, when the universe began. Humans are over 75% water. Water needed its exact qualities so that when it froze it could float keeping the earth from freezing over and, because of earth's distance from the sun, water remains just cool enough, so it doesn't boil away. If protons were not 1,836 times larger than electrons, atoms wouldn't form molecules or us. If the sun was redder or bluer, photosynthesis would not happen, and we would not have the oxygen we need to breath. There are many other variables that had to be precise or this universe would be completely different, and life wouldn't have happened here on earth. The universe appears to have been fine-tuned by God so that we could live. None of this sounds random to me.

How did the ball of energy, matter, information and forces appear out of nothing? Scientist have been making up theories about this for years. Then why did the universe form galaxies, stars, planets, etc.? They tell us that as the universe cooled it caused matter to randomly merge together but it happened uniformly throughout the universe. That is right, the same processes, the same bonds, happened everywhere in the same way. Many have postulated reasons for this. I am here to present the one I accept as true.

I believe that there is one eternal, almighty God that created the universe. So, then who created God? Nobody created God because he has always existed and always will. This idea doesn't make sense to some people because everything, in their opinion, had a beginning and will end. It is understandable why you might draw this conclusion. Human beings are a part of this creation and everything in it had a beginning and will end. That is, everything in this *created universe* had a beginning and will end, naturally. The only way anything could live on is if something supernatural happened that allowed them to emerge on some higher level of existence. So, I went looking for what I had to do to "supernaturally" live on and not die.

First, I asked, "Who is this God that created the universe?" The Bible says that God is love (1 John 4:8). If that is true, then he must be the purest love there could be. This means that entropy could not be a part of God. Entropy is a force that God created to facilitate the life of humans on planet earth and to sustain the universe, so it makes sense that God has no entropy as a part of him. If God is pure love, then, he must always be bonding, multiplying, uniting, creating greater and greater beings and communities of love. Pure love never divides, it always increases, it always creates. Love never compromises who it is but it sends it's love out to others. It means unconditional love, no strings attached.

But why would an eternal God who is pure love create this imperfect universe? Why does this almighty, all knowing, all loving God who is eternal and self-sufficient need or want us? If any of you are parents, you know how much fun and how rewarding children can be. Not always but most of the time. Just like parents want children to love, God, who is pure love, wants his own children to love. He wants to watch his children grow up, mature and discover the wonder of his love. And all he asks is that we love Him in return and love ourselves as we love our neighbors. Real love requires a commitment. I must freely decide to love you. So, if God wanted to create beings who could decide to love him, he needed to create beings with the free will not to.

> "...*without free will there would be no difference between moral and immoral behavior. Since there is, free will must exist.*"
>
> —*Immanuel Kant*

Free will means having the ability and the independence to choose one thing over another. We need to be aware of what we are doing and why, realizing the consequences of the choices we make. Then we weigh our options, doing what is morally and reasonably right or wrong. Based on our character and good judgment, with courage, faith and wisdom, we freely act or refrain from acting.

We are not puppets. We pick what we want and then live with the consequences. The primary reason why God gave us free will was for us to choose love or reject it. Every moment that we are awake, we have the liberty to choose love or to turn our backs on it. It is up to us to decide what we want for our life.

Heaven, God's home, made up of pure love, would not be a place to decide to love. There is no other option in Heaven, you can only love…no entropy there. So, he created a laboratory, we call the universe and, more specifically earth, where humans would have an opportunity to choose love. Is earth the only place he created for living beings to choose love? We don't know for sure but what difference does it make? Suppose there are millions of planets where other beings created "In His Image", get to choose love. That would be a good thing, wouldn't it? For now, the only place we know of or should care about is the one that we are a part of: planet earth.

Free will is the way we get to choose our own salvation. It's logically impossible to *make* someone *freely* do something. Even though God is all-powerful, He won't do something that is morally wrong. He is all-powerful, and he chooses not to force everyone to love him. Given human freedom and human stubbornness, some people may choose not to love but, instead, follow a path towards entropy, destruction, disintegration and decay. God won't force himself on us.

> *"The deepest desire of our hearts is for union with God. God created us for union with himself. This is the original purpose of our lives."*
> —Benjamin Manning

God created the universe as a place where we could choose to love him but not be hard wired to love him. It is entropy that provides the choice. We can love (bond together) or through entropy (divide and separate). We can build or destroy. We can give birth or kill. We can earn what we have or steal it. We have choices. We have "free will" or control over our actions and thoughts. We can determine what we want to do. If we decide not to love God, then we will remain where we are, in our natural state, a combination of love and entropy. In our natural state, we are doomed to go the way of every other natural thing. That is, we will use up all our energy, disintegrate and dissipate as heat. This is the picture of the future that atheists see because they think that a human being is as good as it gets. We are the end of emergence. There is no higher level to emerge onto.

The Human Body Metaphor

After expanding my understanding of God and his role in creation, I wanted to dig deeper into the topic from my Cursillo weekend, "In His Image". I was led to a book entitled "Fearfully and Wonderfully Made" by Phillip Yancy and Dr. Paul Brand. In the preface to the book they write, "...the human body expresses spiritual reality so authentically that soon the common stuff of matter will appear more and more like a mere shadow." Their point is that if we study the human body, mind and spirit we will see that it is a metaphor for reality. I always liked metaphors and analogies and tend to think in pictures. They help me envision the larger reality they represent.

I believe that it is the human soul, not our bodies, that is, "In the Image" of our Creator. Bodies run down, get sick and die and God certainly doesn't, so our bodies do not appear to be in his image. However, in reading about the various systems that make up a human being, there are many lessons that can be learned from our bodies. By studying communities of human cells, tissues, organs and systems, we can draw conclusions about how humans organize into families, communities, workplaces and countries. We can learn from a human being's nervous system. It is its management hierarchy that directs its purpose for living. Humans have an excellent communication department that processes information and measures its progress; muscles that do its work and a distribution department that optimally allocates and disseminates its resources. So, by studying the human body as an analogy of organization, I learned more about how God set up the whole experiment.

As I studied the brain I noticed that it divided its world into distinct categories: Purpose, actions, information processing and resource management. Those categories can be turned into an acronym that is easy to remember: P.A.I.R. To accomplish any *Purpose* (reason why) you need *A.I.R.* (to breathe life into it). You require *Actions* (work) done right (using *Information* to guide you as to how to accomplish the work, track your progress and identify where to find and capture your resources) at the right time and place with the optimal amount of *Resources* I liked the name "PAIR" because it meant joining two together as in love.

Purpose is *why* something exists and, "Why?", has always been my favorite question. Since I was small I always asked why. I debunked the whole Santa Claus thing at five years old. Since purpose is about "why", purpose statements should answer the question *why* someone or something exists. In reviewing several "Purpose Statements", I noticed that they were not answering *why* the person, or the organization existed. Most had more to do with *how* they existed or *what* they intended to do. People don't commit to what you do, they commit to why you do it. Most Purpose Statements defined a current mission statement, not their purpose. Mission is not the same as purpose. The mission is the current attempt to advance the purpose. Mission equals actions, not purpose.

Was this what my vision was about? Was it about developing a useful shortcut to help people find their purpose in life and the actions or mission plans, information and resources needed to make it a reality? At this point in my research, I thought everyone had a different and unique purpose, but I was wrong, we all have the same purpose. It would take more research before I would figure that out.

To discover our true purpose and then to carry it out, we need to understand the reality around us. Defining reality will help us know why we are here so what is real? Reality comes from the Latin root word, "res" meaning "thing". Things like cars, houses, food and clothing can be touched, weighed, measured and they remain basically the same day-to-day. This is the part of reality that is easy to visualize and understand. The real issue is defining the "things" that we can only model through our perceptions, like love and mathematics. We live in a time of polarities. There are those who are convinced that science has all the answers. Others firmly believe that everything taught by the church or written in Holy Scriptures is real and science is wrong. Both groups claim to understand what our existence is all about, but both have only partial explanations.

It would be easier to only accept as true what we physically see, touch and prove but life doesn't work that way. Today much of what we think about must be taken on faith. Faith means believing something is true in the absence of physical evidence. It takes faith to believe in God but it also requires faith to believe in sub-atomic particles because nobody has seen either one of them or can physically prove they exist. Scientists are sure about only four percent of the universe. The other 96 percent consists of black holes, black matter, black energy...in other words, area of the universe that nobody has seen or can prove 100 percent. Mathematical models of reality have predicted sub-atomic particles, black holes and black energy must exist, but nobody has seen any of them. So, for both religion and science, we must trust that what we believe, but cannot see, is real. Science and religion are just two ways of knowing about reality and both require faith. If both require faith, how can people claim that belief in God is a fairy tale but sub-atomic particles are real? Sub-atomic particles cannot be proven by physical evidence but can be believed by the evidence of their actions. I believe in God because of the evidence of His actions.

How about 'awareness'? Is that real? Is that possible? Can I see your point or know what you meant or realize, understand, comprehend or visualize what you are saying, even though you can't point to any physical place where this awareness resides? Yes, because concepts, reasons and meanings are not about cause and effect, so science can't evaluate them. You want to put your whole faith in science but science needs things with no physical characteristics, the things that science can't explain, to draw their scientific conclusions.

Science needs the laws of nature to make its assumptions about the universe but it can't tell you where these laws came from. It believes that the universe is intelligent, follows the laws of nature, but it can't tell you how it does this. It wants us to accept that life, consciousness and rationality are real but intangible and just disappear when we die.

It proclaims that the universe is just a random combination of energy and matter but can't explain codes. Codes include things like written language, musical notes and mathematical equations. They are not random and are developed and created by intelligent consciousness. Isn't its intellectual laziness to write off the laws of nature and codes as unintentional, accidental combinations of symbols that happened without any direction?

The struggle between science and religion has been going on for a long time. Take, for example, Plato who is considered the father of religion and philosophy. He was Aristotle's teacher, but Aristotle disagreed with what Plato taught. He became the father of science. He didn't believe, as Plato did, that there was a spiritual world that was infinitely more real than our earthly one. The two primary branches of thought, science and religion, were born.

Early civilizations, like the Greeks, understood that there were different ways of knowing. The Greeks separated knowledge into two categories: Logos and Mythos and these remain today. Logos, meaning reason, was the practical way that people got along in the world. It was how they improved on their environment and came up with ways to make life better. This way of knowing has evolved into modern day science (left brain thinking). It answers the day-to-day questions of living but does little to help explain the meaning of life.

Mythos, meaning myth, helped the ancient people make sense of a confusing world. Today we argue that myths are not true, but they saw them differently. They supplied meaning to events that Logos, or reason, could not explain. Like a sculpture or a painting, they captured life in unusual but comforting ways that made sense to those who studied it (right brained). So, when the people prayed to the god of war and he drew his sword and cut down a demon, the people felt protected. When a young girl wanted a man to love, she prayed to the goddess of love. Mythos has evolved into modern day religion.

Science is about the *how* and *what* of things while religion is about the *why* and the *meaning* of things. Science can tell us what to do but not what we *should do* or why. Religion is ontological, not scientific, so you can't list all its components and say that this is how it works. On the other hand, science can't tell me if something is true or if my father loves me. The main concept here has to do with the elusive term "being". Some things "are", while others "are not". Why don't we consciously try to work together to understand what is real and true? Finding meaning and purpose through faith in science and religion. Both have things to teach us, but neither have all the answers. Science uses physical proofs through independent verification by impartial third parties used in a logical, rational way to understand reality. However, science also accepts the findings of mathematical models predicting outcomes like ninety-six percent of the universe is dark matter and dark energy that we can't see or independently verify. You can accept something that is unproven because emotionally it feels right, even if there is no other reason or hard evidence to accept it as true. You can choose to believe in invisible, intangible things like love or electrons, while others choose to accept only what they can prove tangibly.

You can know the truth without having the physical evidence to prove it. I could make a valid claim from an established principal that would lead to a reasonable conclusion that is true but can't be proven scientifically. It would be an ontological conclusion but valid, none the less. I can have real feelings or memories when I smell a flower or a certain perfume or think about a childhood Christmas or a beautiful, peaceful sunset without an official scientific explanation of why I feel as I do. I can see colors that stir up emotions within me without any scientific reason to explain it. These things are real even though there is no physical evidence to prove it, so they must be taken on faith.

To Know Truth is To Know Reality

Reality for most of the last six thousand years meant that the earth was controlled by super-human beings called 'gods' that created and controlled everything. It was the gods who protected the world against the forces of 'Chaos' (what we call entropy they called chaos). Religion evolved but the ones in charge of the religion ran the show. In ancient hunter-gather societies, the Shaman, meaning the one who knows, was the only one to contact the spirits in the hidden world.

Civilizations officially began about 5,500 years ago as tribes formed state-level societies. Here religion pervaded every part of life. The pantheon of Greek gods turned into the pantheon of Roman gods once Rome conquered Greece. While these pagan religions were still thriving, changes were underway. Mesopotamia, merged its pantheon of gods together into one god named Marduk. Then Egypt did the same, claiming their one true god was Amun, the giver of life and the one who created the earth and himself. Amun was the forerunner of the Jewish god, Yahweh. Yahweh announced that he was the one true god and there should be no other gods beside him. Then Jesus of Nazareth announced that he was the son of god, the 'way, the truth and the life' (John 14:6) that would lead all to Yahweh forever.

Besides all these changes in religion something else was happening. The field of science was born, and it began as a quest to find the true God. Many of its early pioneers were priests such as Copernicus, George Lenaitre (founder of the Big Bang Theory), George Mendel (founder of genetics). Other prominent Catholics include Galileo, Newton and Leonardo da Vinci. Isaac Newton and Charles Darwin wrote religious books and Catholic tracts.

Over time a rift occurred between the religious and scientific communities. Early scientists, like Rene Descartes, claimed that only things that could be proven without a doubt were real, tangible and believable. God was considered a myth. Science made great advances since Galileo first claimed that the earth revolved around the sun, a proclamation that got him excommunicated from the Catholic

Church. Mathematical laws of gravity, motion, electricity, magnetics emerged. Tremendous progress but science doesn't have all the answers.

> *"Reason doesn't answer every question… To me, reason and faith are twins. They aren't identical twins: they are fraternal twins."*
> —*Albert Einstein*

For all that we know about reality, there is a lot that we don't know. Our five senses are the primary method we use to assess it; filtering out the information we don't deem necessary and sending the important stuff to our brain. Information about color, shapes and movements is processed separately by progressively more complex parts of the brain. Finally, the information is sent to the brain's two hemispheres to form the big picture. It is sent to both because we need the perspective of each one to put it all together. We exist in two states at once: being and becoming. In our "being" state, the brain's right hemisphere, we are the same person today as we were on the day we were born. It guards our purpose for living. Our being state supports our conscious awareness. Some argue that consciousness is a function of the right hemisphere of the brain, but it is not. Consciousness is our soul, our supernatural spirit of love; it is the only part of us that can leave the body at death and move on to eternity. It is not a part of our physical body. I know this from first-hand experience: my spirit left my body on the floor to meet its creator. Our brain's other hemisphere, it's left hemisphere, is our "becoming" self which changes constantly until we die. It is how we develop our character and learn to love. It is where the everyday work of life takes place. The right hemisphere is our "being" self which never changes. It sees reality as the same from the day it was born until now. It is the being state of the brain that tells the becoming state when it is working on the right or the wrong stuff. The two hemispheres are connected by the corpus callosum which transfers motor, sensory, and cognitive information between the hemispheres delivering a complete, three-dimensional picture of our reality.

To fully understand reality, we need to use our whole brain. That means we need the logical, problem solving, scientific left hemisphere of our brain to identify facts and the holistic, synthesizing, intuitive, spiritual right brain to understand their meaning. By putting the two views together we come up with a better understanding of what is true. The science and religious communities could learn from this human metaphor and mimic the brain, combining their two perspectives of reality into one, three-dimensional picture. It makes no sense to limit our perception to books written thousands of years ago, or to only those things that we can physically prove as real.

We Still Don't Have a Consensus about Why We Are Here

There are still many questions to answer. But if science and religion worked together, like our individual brain hemispheres do, we would all have a better understanding of our reality. Scientists say that they can't study love because it is intangible. Are they saying that it is imperceptible, immaterial and unquantifiable? Electrons are also imperceptible, immaterial and difficult to quantify. They have certainly studied electrons and drawn conclusions about them. If scientists look at love as being about uniting, bonding and making two things one they could learn a lot about love that could be passed on to their religious friends. If religious people opened their minds to the concept of emergence, they might understand more about how reality unfolds and how they may emerge on a higher level in Heaven.

Science has studied emergence from the sub-atomic level to the human level. It has documented all the changes along the way. Religion tells us that humans with enough love will emerge on the next level of existence in Heaven. How is this possible? If science and religion work together they may find the God-given mechanism we need to follow to emerge. This could be the most important thing that both religion and science could ever do.

Science calls it consciousness and religion calls it a soul but this is another area where both should be able to collaborate. What is consciousness and how does it function in a human being? Is there a collective unconsciousness between people or can there be conscious awareness on a higher level? It is how we are aware of who we are, the world around us and our place in the universe. Is humanity collectively conscious and is the Earth a living being with consciousness? Is the universe conscious? Since everything in the universe has a purpose what would be the purpose of consciousness beyond the single human being? Lots of questions that require further study and can be done collaboratively.

Are you still uncertain about why we exist? I'm not. God exists, he is the Creator of the universe and he created human beings on earth so that we could consciously decide if we want to love him, ourselves, and our neighbors. The universe is as mortal as we are. It had a beginning and will end. Even if it had universal physical, mental and spiritual traits, it would naturally die like every other created thing that was a part of it. There are those who would argue that the universe is all there is and that it is eternal, but that is not scientifically accurate. There is a scientific consensus that the universe is a closed system that has a limited amount of energy and it cannot accept any more energy from outside itself. All it can do is transform the potential energy it has into kinetic energy that it uses to perform work and finally, the energy gets dissipated as heat and ashes. When all the energy becomes heat and ash, the universe will die. Worshipping the universe is worshipping an idol.

Our purpose is to decide if we want to live with God in Heaven for all eternity. Our mission or action plan is to love as God wants or to pick entropy and die naturally without God. To make a well-informed decision, let's dig deeper into what love and entropy mean and how people use both to live and to die.

CHAPTER 2

What is Entropy?

"If you leave a white post alone, it will soon be a black post."

—*G. K. Chesterton*

Since the time of the Big Bang, the entire universe has experienced a natural, downward spiral towards disorder and chaos. The reason for this, as we said earlier, is the Second Law of Thermodynamics; better known as *entropy*. It was first defined by Sadi Carnot in 1824. Energy is the capacity of a system to work and entropy is the waste product of that work.

"Entropy" is derived from the Greek word for "a turning towards". It is turning towards destruction and is "turning away from" love. It is running down the universal stairs to destruction. As we move through time, the second law of thermodynamics states that the entropy of an isolated system (like our universe) tends to increase; it will not decrease. Its primary trait is irreversibility. Entropy is thought of as a kind of clock for the universe. It has been called the "Arrow of Time" because everything it touches moves from greater order and oneness to greater disorder over time. The higher the entropy, the lower the probability of order.

Our universe is expanding like a balloon being blown up. There are those who say that, at some point, it will stop expanding and start contracting. If that were to happen, they argue, time would go the

21

other way and things (including us) would get younger and newer. This kind of intellectual speculation is a waste of "time". It is like saying gravity holds you to the surface of the earth but someday it won't. The universe has specific laws and forces at play and we must live with them, not imagine changing them. Instead, we need to change our view of reality to one that fits with what is real.

Entropy is our natural state. We need it to breathe, eat and stay alive but if we allow it to control us, we will not have enough love to emerge in Heaven. We need to improve the ratio of love to entropy. The greater the nominator (love), and the smaller the denominator (entropy), the greater the chance to emerge (Love/Entropy). So, first let's recognize how entropy affects and "infects" our life and then let's learn how love can be its antidote. Spotting entropy and evaluating whether it is a positive or negative force in a given situation is the key skill we need to develop. How we battle the ill effects of entropy with love is the subject of our next chapter.

It shouldn't surprise you to learn that entropy is a word that means many things and, as a result, causes confusion and chaos. It has been used to measure how uniform the distribution of energy is, the availability of energy, the probability of order in a system. It has also been used to measure the natural decay in a social system or in describing the breakdown of information. There is, however, a common thread in all these definitions: they all are the opposite of unity, order and love. Instead of building relationships, good communication, bringing others together, creating order and life; entropy leads to separation, miscommunication, disorder and death. If the manifestations of entropy are the opponent of love, why aren't we focused on routing entropy out of our lives? The Hindu word "Adharma" is a good definition of entropy. Even the word sounds like to "add harm".

Hindu word, "Adharma"—Absence of dharma (purpose).
Chaos (entropy)

From the beginning, entropy, has been an unstoppable force that is breaking things down, making things fall apart, destroying, wreaking havoc and killing. All exchanges of energy are subject to inefficiencies such as friction or radioactive heat loss, which increases the entropy of a system. It is converting all the potential energy in the universe into unusable heat, spreading the energy out and then, as its final act, killing off everything. Entropy keeps the universe and everything in it in a state of disequilibrium as it converts potential energy into spent energy. When it uses up all the potential energy, activity will stop leaving the universe in a steady state or equilibrium (dead as a door nail). Anyone who believes in an eternal universe or in endless reincarnations or that the "universal mind" is the real supreme being is wrong and entropy is the reason why.

Entropy, not hate, is opposite of love. Hate means a strong dislike or ill will toward persons or things. Hate is the absence of love just like cold is the absence of heat. Evil is the absence of goodness and silence is the absence sound. The difference is that entropy is real, it is not just the absence of something else. Entropy always destroys and kills, and you can hate without destroying or killing the subject of your hate. Entropy will be responsible for the death of all things in this universe including hate. Entropy is the "original sin" that was built into the universe. It is with us from the moment of conception to our physical death. Even after death, it is there to break down and destroy our physical body. Unlike hate, entropy can be scientifically measured like mass, momentum and energy. It is behind the separation of every baby from its mother, every divorce and every physical death. Every time you fight with a neighbor, have a car accident or repaint your peeling house, entropy is there working against you.

Entropy will cause metal to rust and rust cost more than all other natural disasters combined. It costs the US government three percent of its gross national product or $440 billion annually. It threatens our health, safety, security, environment and future. Rust causes corrosion which gnaws away at any metal. Corrosion is a pervasive enemy that never rests. Rust is a physical reminder of how damaging entropy can be. Mountains are powerless against entropy: erosion, wind, water and acids caused the Grand Canyon by dissolving miles of rock.

An easy way to remember entropy is to think of one thing becoming two. It turns anything with potential energy (one) into usable energy and heat (two). Think of entropy like a log you would put in a fireplace. It begins full of potential energy. You light it and it does its work, burning to create the light and heat of the fire, and finally, it is reduced to useless ashes when entropy dissipates it as heat. This is the same way that entropy works on all energy sources. Everything in the universe is subject to the Second Law of Thermodynamics but entropy is flawed, not perfect like God. Its flaws will be its undoing. It will end in what others might call Hell, Hades, Gahanna and some similar name but it means the same thing: heat death. This is how the plan was set up by the Creator. So, the "normal" condition of things in the universe is moving from greater order to lesser order over time. This means things are breaking down, breaking apart, becoming diseased, disintegrating, and dying according to His plan. So, when you see these things, it isn't God punishing anyone, it is time passing as designed. The universe is on a timer (God's timer) and it is winding down. It was designed to be a temporary place for us to choose love. Choose now, you don't know when the timer will go off. God is perfect love; the opposite of entropy. Instead of breaking things down, He is eternal unity. Instead of disease, his love brings health. Instead of disintegrating, he is integrating. Instead of chaos, his love produces order. Instead of dying, life. When we move towards him we feel his love because we are living according to His will. He wants us to be one with him in eternity as a husband is one with his bride. When we turn away from Him, entropy kicks in, or sin if you prefer the term, and our problems pile up.

Sin, or entropy, is the thief that puts something else ahead of our love for God, neighbor and self. The Hebrew word for sin is "to diminish" which is a synonym for entropy. Love of things, ideas, places, money or…anything else that you value *more than* God, your neighbor or yourself, is sin or entropy. That doesn't mean you can't "love" other things but just know their place. You just need to keep your priorities straight.

We live in a world with too many choices and too many distractions: in short, too much entropy. You have heard the term, "Analysis/Paralysis". With so many choices, we end up doing nothing because we freeze. Instead of finding ways to work and play together, we keep looking for ways to differentiate ourselves, separate and disconnect from others. We are obsessed with hoarding money, accumulating toys, building walls and gating ourselves off from our neighbors. We buy home security and video monitoring systems because we are afraid somebody might steal our stuff or kidnap us. We purchase identity theft protection and get every kind of insurance under the sun because we think that everyone and everything is out to get us. The Bible has 500 verses on prayer and 2,350 verses on how to handle money and possessions. Apparently, the Bible authors recognized our problem with material things and trust.

> *"The ego tends to equate having with being. I have therefore I am. And the more I have, the more I am. The ego lives through comparison. How you are seen by others turns into how you see yourself."*
> —A New Earth, page 45

Are we human *beings* or human *doers*? We are beings and being has to do with our souls, not with our physical possessions. What we have comes from what we do. These may be necessary parts of life, but they must be balanced by time spent being. One time a wealthy man approached Jesus and said that he tried to do everything right in his life. Jesus told him to sell all he had and follow him. The man couldn't do that and walked away dejected. Jesus doesn't ask everyone to give up all they possess but he knew that this man needed to do that to save his soul. Eventually, entropy will cause your muscles to atrophy, arteries to clog, bones to break, and stress and fear will cause your mental and physical health to deteriorate. It may affect your heart, suppress your immune system and disrupt your digestion and production of hormones. It may cause anxiety and fear that can kill the brain's capacity to learn and result in panic, physical illness and disease. Entropy corrodes right down to our cellular level. When cells fail to connect, or relate to the cells around them, they have no purpose to exist, so they die, or they go rogue and become cancerous.

Cancer is a "generic" name we give to many different types of the disease. It can start in any of the trillions of cells in our bodies.

Normal cells are very distinct types of cells with specific functions; cancer cells are not. They just keep dividing without stopping, grabbing the nutrients of the healthy cells, not specializing in anything. They may form tumors that are malignant and invade nearby cells and organs. Then they can break off and travel through the blood or lymph systems to infect other parts of the body. Cancer cells ignore signals that tell normal cells to stop dividing or die. The cancer controls increasing amounts of the bodies resources until it kills the host. By being selfish, disobedient, sneaky and being rule breakers, cancer cells eventually kill the body that gave them life and nutrition. This is an excellent example of how entropy can get out of control, damage or kill its host whether the host is an individual, an organization or a national government.

One cancer affecting families is the retreat from getting married. People are marrying much later or not at all. Some claim they can't handle their own lives let alone be responsible for a spouse and children. Other admit they are too selfish to care for anyone but themselves. Unemployment, under employment and poverty suppresses people from wanting to marry. A lack of community leads to less marriages. Without the community support structure, raising families becomes too difficult for many. The sexual revolution and women's movement have contributed to a downturn in marriages.

> *"In 1970, the U.S. Census Bureau determined a house filled with married parents and their children under eighteen years constituted 40 percent of all households. By 2012 that number had fallen to 20 percent. In 1960, 72 percent of all adults were married. By 2016, it was half. In 1965, 17 percent of all adults were married. By 2016, it was only half. In 1965, 17 percent of adults aged twenty-one to thirty-five were never married. In 2017, the never-married number was 57 percent... About 40 percent of all children born in 2016 were born out of wedlock (which marks a slight improvement). A related trend is childless women. In 1976 about one*

in three women of childbearing age was childless (35 percent). In 2016, nearly half were (49 percent)… About one in six Americans said marriage is an outdate institution, in one 2017 poll."
—Alienated America, P 67

When you selfishly care more about yourself than anyone else you open the door to further entropy. The Apostle Paul called this the "works of the flesh" and said they are opposed to the spirit (of love) when He said to the Galatians (5: 19-21) "Now the works of the flesh are obvious immorality, impurity, licentiousness, idolatry, sorcery, hatreds, rivalry, jealousy, outbursts of fury, acts of selfishness, dissensions, factions, occasions of envy, drinking bouts, orgies, and the like. I warn you, as I warned you before, that those who do such things will not inherit the kingdom of God."

The kingdom of God is the kingdom of love because God is love and His kingdom is love. So, if you let entropy rule your life, as Paul says, you will not inherit the kingdom of love. All these actions are entropic and work against love so if you are engaged in these acts, you will be blocking love from growing in you. As if these are not bad enough, extreme entropy leads to violent crimes like murder, rape and aggravated assault; property crimes like stealing money, jewelry, vehicles, electronics and firearms; and terrorism on a global scale, wars, nuclear proliferation, failed nation-states and hoarding of resources by the few while the many starve. All of these are ways that entropy breaks things apart destroying us and our civilization. It is cancer on a larger scale. We need to learn all we can about entropy so that we can recognize it when we see it and then liberally apply its remedy, love.

Joseph Tainter, an American anthropologist and historian, studied twenty-four civilizations that have collapsed over the last six thousand years. He described why they failed, and although he didn't use the term entropy, it was the reason they broke down. Each society became more and more complex and chaotic (another name entropy). Each civilization collapsed when it could no longer sustain these complex systems. Over taxed, over regulated, over emphasis on special interests all causing complexity and chaos leading to each civilization's downfall. Our civilization is becoming more and more complex and chaotic now so how long can it survive without us making the necessary changes?

> *"...social disintegration—the progressive unraveling of the human connections that give life structure and meaning: declining attachment to work; declining participation in community life; declining rates of marriage and two-parent child-rearing."*
> —Alienating America, P 101

Spotting Entropy in Action

One of entropy's favorite weapons is misdirection: sending you to a different place than you intended to go. How does this cause destruction? If you were heading down the wrong road and a sign pointed you in the direction you wanted to go but the sign was incorrect, you would get further and further away from where you intended to go. If you were doing something that was destroying your family, and someone convinced you to do something that would make it even worse but told you it would make it better, that would be misdirection in action.

It is the basis of every magic act. You see what you believe, or *think*, is happening while the magician secretly does something else. It may have the appearance of being true, but it is not. I learned about this concept in a business seminar I attended. It was called, "Hidden Agendas". The idea was that people say one thing when they mean something different. The case study was a town meeting. We broke up into two "parties" to vote on a new town ordinance. We were given the real reason why we wanted the ordinance to pass and were told that we couldn't let the other side know. We had to come up with a plausible argument for passing it without letting our opponents know our real motivation. I learned a lot about how people can hide their true thoughts through misdirection like when our politicians in Washington, D.C. talk. It is almost impossible to understand where they are coming from half the time. Thanks to video tapes we get to see them talking out of both sides of their mouths. They were in favor of a wall on our southern border a few years ago and oppose it now as inhumane. What changed? The President said he wanted the wall, so now they don't.

The internet can be helpful, but it also can be a tool of misdirection. Even though it has many benefits like instant access to information and easy connections to people, it can also be very good at misdirecting us. You could waste hours on the net instead of taking care of your physical and mental health and paying attention to others. Some use it to bully others. Some text while they drive and cause accidents. Some become addicted to pornography or buying material things advertised on it. It can be good, but it also can be dangerous. The internet is only a tool, it is not a force for love or entropy even though both can use it to advance their cause. Step back and think about how you are using it.

There are many variations of entropy's misdirection like a cheating spouse, a shoplifter, a con artist, the "friend" that steals from you when you're not looking or the politician that promises the world with no real intention of delivering on his promises. Those who judge people for the things they do, while they are doing far worse themselves. People lie, exaggerate and point you in the wrong direction all the time. These are all ways to seduce you into thinking one thing is happening when really something else is going on.

There are so many distractions and propaganda (such as fake news) that it is becoming more difficult to discern the truth. The average American only reads about nineteen minutes a day and young people are reading far less than the national average. During the presidential election of 2016, forty-four percent of adults got their unfiltered and unedited news from social media. So how many voters cast their ballots because of some fake news report they heard about the other candidate? Fake news is not the way to make informed decisions.

Entropy is ripping apart our written and broadcast news sources. Americans are so polarized they have no interest in reading or learning what the "opposition" has to say. When people share what they read, it is a sign of togetherness. To meaningfully engage, there must be a certain amount of common knowledge about the subject. With so many unreliable sources of information out there today, it is driving a wedge between us. Sharing ideas glues us together as a nation (a loving action). Multi-culturalism, multi-language communities and too many information sources are working to undermine our shared life. There are roughly 6,800 languages spoken in the world today. If we don't share our language with others, we have a harder time uniting with them for the common good. Freedom of discourse and debate about the big ideas of life, death, and meaning is what made America great. Today people who make their opinions known get shouted down or threatened. We need to engage with those who think differently, not build barriers or only listen to those who think like us.

Another powerful weapon of entropy is fear. Fear projects the future and imagines the worse possible outcome. Worry, fear's companion, can drain your energy, make you angry and even sick. As Jesus said, today has enough concerns. Take care of tomorrow's problems tomorrow. God never gives us more than we can handle and does what is best for us. If you believe this, you will have His peace which surpasses all understanding.

Maybe an example of what we have been discussing will make things clearer. Saul Alinsky was a community organizer who died in 1972. He promoted revolution in America to destroy a system that he regarded as oppressive and unjust. His goal was to overturn American society to build a new, "more equitable" nation on its ashes. He believed that mankind was divided into three parts: the haves, the have nots and the have a little but want more. In his book, Rules For Radicals, he included Lucifer in his dedication:

> *"Lest we forget at least an over-the-shoulder acknowledgement to the very first radical: from all our legends, mythology, and history (and who is to know where mythology leaves off and history begins—or which is which), the first radical known*

to man who rebelled against the establishment and did it so effectively that he at least won his own kingdom—Lucifer."

—Saul Alinsky

Alinsky praises Lucifer because he believed "the end justifies the means". He said one man's positive was another man's negative. He was in favor of doing what you can with what you have while clothing it in moral garments (misdirection). Those who were not with him, were against him. Inequitable distribution of wealth was immoral. He emphasized the need for disorganization, disruption and chaos (entropy). To him, the illusion of power was as effective as actual power. He said profess one system of morality but live another (misdirection). Ridiculing his opponents was one of his favorite weapons. Like the Bolsheviks who revolted in favor of Communism, he advocated for a peaceful revolt from Capitalism to a Utopian Socialism. In his perfect world all would be equal and there would be no need for God. In his mind, if you pushed a negative long enough it would become a positive. Constant class warfare (entropy) advanced his cause. He would pick a target, freeze it, personalize it, and polarize it turning as many people as possible against it. It was easier to attack a person, an organization or an idea if you put a face on it.

Alinsky, the poster boy for entropy, was just one of the people trying to undermine our way of life. We need to be vigilant and uncover the ways that entropy is attacking us. The problem is escalating like raging waters and we need to be the dams that stop it from surging. We can't be that frog that is placed in warm water and dies because he doesn't feel the temperature rising until it boils and kills him. If he only recognized what was happening, he could have jumped out and saved his life. We still have time to jump out of entropy's boiling pot and save our lives.

Entropy is rampart in the United States today. Entropy causes excessive loneliness leading to suicide and opioid overdose deaths. Alienated individuals have lost interest in participating in the social order. Communities are being pulled apart by people who self-segregate based on their income, ethnic background and education: the highly educated and successful cluster together away from the rest of society. The poorly educated and underemployed are forced to live together in poorer sections of town. A lack of opportunity and participation has caused a large increase in the amount of incarcerations and homelessness. Self-centeredness leads to people waiting to marry or not marrying at all, higher divorce rates and illegitimacy. A lack of motivation results in more high school and workforce dropouts, unemployment, and excessive drug and alcohol use. Less human contact from the overuse of electronics leads to lower participation in sports, neighborhoods associations, church, social and civic clubs and involvement in local, state and federal politics.

> *"At the root of the most significant problems America faces at home is the weakening of our core institutions—family and community, church and school, business and labor associations, civic and fraternal organizations."*
> —Alienated America, page 12

Positive Entropy

For all the damage that negative entropy causes, is it any wonder why people say that no *"loving God"* would ever have created such a destructive force. As it turns out, though, entropy is an essential part of God's plan for the universe. Without it, we would not be here.

Every human being consists of about 10 quadrillion human cells and another 100quadrillion bacterium cells. We couldn't survive a day without bacteria performing its many *entropic* duties.

> *"Before a single plant or animal appeared on earth, bacteria invented all of life's essential chemical systems. They transformed the earth's atmosphere, developed a way to get energy from the sun, devised the first bioelectrical systems, invented sex and locomotion, worked out the genetic machinery, and*

learned how to merge and organize into new and higher collectives. These are ancestors to be proud of!"
—The Way Life Works, p 2

Bacteria, an agent of entropy, breaks down the food we eat, extracting nutrients and making them available to us. Bacteria also defends against infections and toxins. We could not move, digest, think, feel or perform most bodily functions without the energy we get from breaking the chemical bonds in the food (sugar) molecules that we eat. Metabolism is a positive form of entropy. It is from the Greek word meaning "exchange". Entropy extracts or "exchanges" usable nutrients, highly concentrated energy, from the oxidation of food or it or it gets the nutrients from substances, such as fat, stored in our bodies. Enzymes digest the food and break it down to its basic building blocks: glucose, amino acids and fatty acids. Then they are absorbed into the bloodstream and distributed throughout the body. The end-product of metabolism is entropy: highly defused wasted heat.

Humans are made up of atoms, that bond together to form simple molecules and they bond together to form chain molecules, then molecular structures, cells, cellular communities (tissues), and systems (all loving actions). It takes a certain amount of energy to make the bond and then through entropy the rest gets disbursed as heat. If some of the energy was not disbursed as heat, there would be enough energy to return and destroy the bonds that were just made. Since some of the energy used to make the bond is now useless heat, there isn't enough energy to break the bonds. Without the bonds, we wouldn't be here.

Unless plants were created and produced sugar and oxygen, the waste product of sugar making, we wouldn't be here. Entropy extracts the oxygen from the plants and without it we couldn't breathe. Positive entropy includes capturing energy and matter from outside the body, taking it in, breaking it down and transferring it to do the work of growing, adapting and living. Raw energy gets broken down and is transformed into a more useful state or else it passes through our bodies adding nothing.

All energy that enters the earth's biosphere eventually leaves it as heat. Green plants capture the energy from sunlight and chemically bond it to sugar—life's universal food—through photosynthesis. Then herbivores (plant eaters) get their sugar from eating the plants and carnivores (meat eaters) get their sugar from the flesh of the herbivores. And finally, the decomposers (mostly bacteria and fungi) get their sugar from breaking down the waste products and dead bodies of the other three groups. All require entropy to function.

Human beings, like all living systems, are essentially energy processing systems. A woman's egg needs entropy to accept the sperm, then to divide a few million times creating her newborn child. Every living being, including humans, needs entropy or it dies. Living beings are open systems. We take in free energy from our environment, process it, use it to perform actions (work) or store it for future use and expel the entropy that it causes. This process allows living systems to grow, change, adapt, and self-renew. All the thousands of biochemical systems that run our bodies are maintained and regulated by feedback systems (information processing systems run by entropy). We must continually locate and take in external data, break it down into discardable, useless data or useful information that can be distributed to where it is needed in the body or stored for future use. If we can't find the right information from the external environment we have to locate it in substances stored within us such as memories. The entropic information allocation processes, like energy processing, is essential to our survival.

Entropy protects the human body by going to war on alien microbes that attack it. It also creates pain that can be directional, pointing out areas that need special attention. It causes us to experience ordeals, temptations, and challenges that teach us how to be better people. It is behind your urge for independence, self-reliance and self-sufficiency.

The Big Bang was an act of entropy. Arthur Edenton called entropy the "Supreme Law of Nature". Entropy is behind the chaos, instability and freedom that provides the right conditions for higher life forms to emerge. It unleashes the carbon dioxide that plants need to produce the oxygen that we, in turn, need to live. It processes our waste products, keeping us healthy, and makes the waste useful. It synthesizes vitamins and amino acids. Entropy breaks down and eliminates impurities in our water and soil. It puts some carbons under tremendous heat and pressure turning them into diamonds, some heavy metals into precious metals like gold and some sand into pearls.

So, despite all its negatives, entropy can cause positive thing to happen. It is an essential part of God's original universal plan. It is a tool nature uses to create and sustain our lives. Since its primary job is tearing things down, breaking them up, separating things and undoing bonds, it can be helpful on a local level but on a larger scale it still is our primary enemy. The large-scale effects of entropy are the ones that people point to saying, "How can a loving God allow these things to happen?" It is a necessary part of the universe and it gets blamed for many things that happen because of our own poor decisions. Most of the worse diseases that plague us today are induced by poor health choices. For instance, if we choose to smoke, we risk contracting lung cancer. If we overeat or allow stress to overtake us, we may cause a heart attack, a stroke or diabetes. This is not God's choice, it is ours.

The mechanisms that control entropy are the same for little, positive things as they are for bigger, negative things. The same rules apply. We would not be here without entropy. We can learn from it and use it for our own benefit. If we can spot entropy in action, we can judge whether it is operating in a positive or negative way. Once we do this, we can decide to offset it with more love or let it do its work.

CHAPTER 3

―――⁂―――

What is Love?

*"At the end of our days on this earth, after all our
successes and failures, the measure of worth for our
life will be how much we have loved."*

—Ammachi

"Negative entropy" is the source of all disunity, disintegration, disorder, destruction and even death. It will eventually kill every object in its path. How do we stop it or, at least, slow down its reign of terror? We need to counter its destructive force with one that unites, brings parts together and builds and creates order. This force is love. Like the Beatles sang, "All you need is love…" Dr. Ashley Montagu claimed that, "Love is the only force that keeps us from destroying each other". "Love alone is capable of uniting living beings in such a way as to complete and fulfill them.", according to Pierre Teilhard de Chardin. But what is love? It is an overused and misunderstood concept. It means different things to different people. You don't love your automobile the same way that you love your children. You don't love your dog the way you love your mother. Many times, when we say "love" we really mean "like". There are many forms of love, all of them different but all of them love. Kindness, patience, forgiveness are all forms of love as is honesty, generosity and humility. Love comes in many shapes and sizes. It is about connecting with another whether it is a spouse, child, dog or the New England Patriots (either you love them or hate them). Every act of goodness, justice, sacrifice or helping the needy, is an act of love.

The English language has only one word for love, but it can mean many different things. Love can be platonic, flirtatious, sexual, or unconditional. Is it any wonder that we have trouble defining the concept of love? It is such an overused term that many feel funny even saying it today or they say it so much that it loses its meaning. All this confusion about the definition of love feeds into the hands of the enemy. Entropy "loves" to divide, obscure and conquer. If it can make you doubt you are experiencing love or wonder about what it means to love, and which type of love you are experiencing; then it can confuse you and poison your love with lust. Lust is not real love. It is the desire for the love that belongs to someone else. Seek love, not lust.

> (Humans are) "a species wired for love kindness, and compassion... The larger, unreported story of the human species is our desire to connect and cooperate, to give and receive love."
> —The Empathic Civilization, Jeremy Rifkin

Love has many forms like selfless giving expecting nothing in return or forgiving wrongs. It includes caring for the weak, vulnerable, poor and needy. It gives to others but also returns many good things such as more friends, closer family ties, happier and healthier lives, better marriages and jobs. Love is a value exchange. That means you give and receive love, hopefully, in equal measure. Think of it like the scales of justice. If you are constantly piling your love on one side of the scale and the person on the other end is not putting any love on her side, then there is an unequal value exchange. You are doing all the giving and getting nothing in return. This is unconditional love, but it is not the kind of love that humans desire. I want to give you as much love as you give back to me. When our scale of love is balanced and we both feel like we are exchanging a fair amount of love with each other.

Study love; learn how to expand your love connections. Love creates, multiplies, it doesn't destroy or divide. It is not lost when it is given away, you retain your love even if you give it to hundreds like the wise teacher who tells his students all he knows but retains all that he taught. We *share* the love and knowledge we possess but do not give them away.

Love leads to greater unity, order and oneness. It helps us grow, learn, change and adapt. Through love we communicate our wants and needs to each other. It is this spirit of love that causes us to strive to be better, more creative, inspired and wise. It gives us the urge to be more loving, to transform and transcend our human condition putting us on the path back to God for all eternity. Love leads to social cohesion, cooperation and growth in relationships at all levels.

What Kind of Love Does God Require?

Which kind of love did the Bible writers mean? When the Bible was written, Greek was the predominant language. The Greeks had many definitions for love, but they had separate words to describe each type of love: storge, eros, philia and agape. Storge referred to a physical affection or the love of family and close friends. Eros was about satisfying physical or sexual desire and intercourse. It can be the most selfish type of love and can easily slip into lust. Philia, is brotherly love, a dispassionate kind of virtuous love. It refers to friendly affection. The highest form of love was called agape. It is self-sacrificing, voluntary and unconditional love. This is the kind of willful, volitional, unconditional love that one chooses with free will. It is love that is based on an aware, conscious and deliberate decision. The New Testament uses agape love in many places and philia in others.

When the Pharisees asked Jesus which commandment of all the ones passed down to them by their fore-fathers, was the most important? Jesus knew they were trying to trip him up. There were 613 commandments in the Old Testament, so which would he choose? He didn't hesitate, splicing together two passages from the Torah: "You shall love the Lord, your God, with all your heart, with all your soul, and with all your strength" (Deuteronomy 6:5). "This is the greatest and first commandment. The second is like it: 'You shall love your neighbor as yourself.' (Leviticus 19:18). *He promised that if they followed these two commandments, they would be with God in Heaven for all eternity.* Of all the commandments, he boiled it down to loving enough to emerge in Heaven. The temple priests at that time had over 400 distinct rituals they performed daily to fulfill their holy duties and 1,521 things you couldn't do on the Sabbath and Jesus said love was enough. No wonder they didn't like Him.

Suppose you were offered a new job. Your boss told you, "Follow these two simple rules and you will excel in this company. Surpass them and you will be promoted to the next higher level." You would study the two rules and be sure to follow them faithfully. Asking others for advice and researching the company manuals, papers and presentations that explained how to better carry out the two rules. You would seek out mentors that have performed the two rules well. You would put all your effort into outdoing the requirements in the hopes of gaining that promotion to next level. Does what I just said sound like a wise approach if you wanted to do well in your job? If you would do all that to perform the duties of your job, why wouldn't you do the same with your life?

So, just as the boss told the new hire, "Follow these two rules and you will do well in your job and get promoted." Jesus (our boss) told us, "Just follow these two rules and you will do well in this life and get promoted (to Heaven). Sounds simple enough. Why aren't more people spending their time learning how to do this? Why are more people like the Pharisees who count the number of rituals they follow instead of the love they share? Rituals will not allow us to emerge, only love will.

The strict followers of Jewish law were furious at Jesus' answer. These two root commandments were precisely the ones they kept breaking. Observance of the law for them was not an act of divine love but rather of self-promotion; a way to keep score. Rather than their adherence to the law leading to love of neighbor, it led to judging neighbors who failed to live up to their standards. Paul, the converted Pharisee, said: "If I speak in human or angelic tongues, but do not have love, I am a resounding gong or a clashing cymbal."

(1 Corinthians 13:1). Paul knew this from experience. To this day, there are still many "Pharisees" that legalistically judge the followers of Jesus.

The verse from Leviticus 19:18, "You shall love your neighbor as yourself", only referred to fellow Israelites, not the people in neighboring nations. As he often did, Jesus expanded the original meaning to outsiders when he told the story about the Good Samaritan (Luke 10: 25-37). It is the story of a robbery with the victim left bleeding, beaten, stripped and dying on the side of the road. Prominent Jews, a priest and a Levite, ignored him while a Samaritan, a foreigner, stopped to help. It was the Samaritan who showed this stranger love by helping him to safety at a nearby inn. He cared for him and when he had to leave, he paid the innkeeper to watch over him until he was better. The Samaritans were considered enemies of the Jews, but Jesus called them neighbors and said that we should love them and do as this man did.

Paul states that faith, hope and love are important but the most important is love. When we die, we can leave faith behind because we will instantly meet Jesus (with physical evidence of God we would no longer need faith) and if He opens the gates of Heaven to us, we can leave hope behind because we will have achieved our hoped-for purpose. The one virtue we will not leave behind is our love. This we will take with us and based on how much love we have, determine our starting point in our Heavenly exploration about what God's pure love means.

God is love but human love is not the same as God's

Pure love is too mighty to define and since we have entropy in this universe nothing in it can be one hundred percent pure love. There is much more to pure love than we can ever know with our limited human capacity to love. The American Heritage Dictionary defines love as "an intense affection for another person based on familial or personal ties". Often this "intense affection" stems from a sexual attraction for that other person. We love other people, or we say we love other people, when we are attracted to them and when they make us feel good. Notice that a key phrase in the dictionary definition of love is the phrase "based on". This phrase implies that we love *conditionally*; in other words, we love someone because they fulfill a need that we want fulfilled before we can love them. How many times have you heard it said, "I love you because you are beautiful;" or "I love you because you take good care of me;" or "I love you because you make me laugh." Each of these reasons are conditional love. Love me, and I'll love you.

Human love is not only conditional, it is emotional and impulsive. We love based on feelings that can change from one moment to the next. The divorce rate is extremely high today because husbands and wives claim that they "fall out of love". They may go through a rough patch in their marriage, and they no longer "feel" love for their spouse, so they call it quits. Evidently, they believe that their marriage vow of "till death do us part" means they can part at the death of their feelings of love for their spouse rather than at their physical death.

> *"At the core of the teachings of all mystical traditions whether indigenous, Christian, Jewish, Buddhist, Hindu, or Sufism—is one simple, consistent principle: love."*
> —Life's Operating Manual,
> Tom Shadyac, p236

God created man with two basic desires: the desired to be loved and the desire to love. God's love is unconditional, and unemotional. He doesn't love us because we're lovable or because we make Him feel good; he loves us because he is love. He created us to have a loving relationship with Him, and He sacrificed His Son, Jesus, (who was willing to die for us) to restore that relationship. God says love is unconditional and sacrificial, and it's not based on feelings. To understand what true love is and to be able to truly love others, we have to learn more about God, and we can do this through a close personal relationship with Him by putting our faith in Jesus Christ, who was God's sacrifice of love for us and by calling on His Holy Spirit of Love to guide us in the way we should live today.

Wait. If God's love is unconditional, why did Jesus have to die on the cross to restore our relationship with God? That sounds like conditional love. Well, suppose you were stuck in a cave and could not find your way out and you might die there. You could think of how perfect life could be outside the cave but if you couldn't get to it, you would be without hope. Then suppose someone from outside of the cave came to you and said he can show you the way out of the cave if you followed him. The only problem was that there was an avalanche and your guide had to go first to make sure he could break through to the other side. He goes ahead and appears to fall to his death. Again, you are hopelessly stuck without a way out. Then he reappears and tells you he has cleared the way to the outside and it is magnificent. All you need to do is follow his path and you will safely get to the promised land outside. So, this guide becomes your "way, truth and life" line to the other side. The outside didn't change. You needed help to get there and, fortunately, someone from the outside came to show you the way. Jesus is that guide. He restored the way to Heaven because humanity couldn't find the way on its own. God's acceptance of you (from the cave) is still unconditional. However, you need to make the effort to get there. Jesus provided the way. God's love never changed, just your effort to react to that love.

Mankind is separated from God and longs be united with Him forever. Our need "to be loved" can only be fulfilled by our knowing that God loves us with unconditional love. This is what gives us our security and our *identity* in this life. Our need "to love" can be fulfilled only by our learning to love God, ourselves and others in the way that He desires. As Jesus said, "Love one another as I love you." (John 15: 12). (I hope he didn't mean get crucified) This is what will give our lives meaning and what will allow us to emerge in Heaven.

Can anyone really comprehend "unconditional" love? It seems that the love parents have for their children is as close to unconditional love as we can get in this world. Parents continue to love their children through good times and bad and don't stop loving them if they don't meet their expectations. We make a choice to love our children even when others consider them unlovable; our love doesn't stop when we don't "feel" love for them or receive love from them. This is like God's love for us but God's love is much greater, and it transcends any possible human definition of love. We are commanded to love so what do we do? We love, or we can't move on.

Defining God (like that is possible)

God is the creator of the universe. He is not physically or mentally a part of it. It is not him but a separate thing he created made from energy and matter. So, if He is in it at all, it must be His spirit of love that is in it (better known as the Holy Spirit). He is uncreated, eternal and always was and always will be (I use the term, "He" because *he* is the initiator of the universe and the space *he* created is the receptor or the female of the story). Think of it like a male plug in a female electrical socket—it may be a crude analogy, but it does describe the relationship. For some, it is difficult to believe that He always was and is uncreated. Everything we know was created and has a set "life span" because the only reality we have ever experienced is the created universe.

Everything in this universe began and will end. But He is the creator of the universe who doesn't have to follow the universe's rules. Everything in this universe that has a beginning must have begun from something or someone else. So, paraphrasing Thomas Aquinas; there must be something or someone that does not have a beginning that is behind the whole thing. The one who made up the rules doesn't have to follow them himself.

Why do we think we could possibly know all there is to know about God? If you were inside a dark, sealed box, how could you explain what is happening outside the box? We are in the "box", the universe, and cannot know what is happening outside of the box until we are freed from it when we die. Jesus jumped into the box and provided valuable information about what we needed to do to get out of the box if we just listen to his directions.

When Moses asked God, what His name was, He said Yahweh, meaning "I Am that I Am"; I continually exist. In other words, He is and always was as the Hebrew translation says, "underived existence". He didn't give His name because He doesn't need a name, He is the only God. We use names to distinguish one being or thing from another, like this is a person and that is a rock. In Jewish thought, a name is not merely an arbitrary designation or a random combination of sounds. The name conveys the nature, essence, history and reputation of the one named. People often refer to a person's "good name". When a business is sold, it frequently includes "goodwill" which is the value of the company's "good name". The Hebrew concept of a name is very similar to these ideas. So, it was a very unexpected answer when He said He doesn't need a name just a description of who He is: underived existence, creator of the universe and pure love.

If God is pure love than he must be nothing but love. However, he has been described in many other ways such as perfect, supreme, almighty, omnipresent, omnipotent, just and true. If he is infinitely wise, true, beautiful and just then he is pure love and wisdom, truth, beauty and justice are just some of the ways to describe His pure love. We can string together many adjectives to describe Him but there are no appropriate words to describe Him completely. God is a boundless, infinite, all-encompassing love so immense that he can't be contained or fully explained.

> *"Language can be a window through which we glimpse God but never a box in which God can be contained."*
> —C. S. Lewis

Of all the words to describe him, John's portrayal is the simplest and the most elegant, "God is love" (1 John 4: 16). Simply love, as if love is simple. He is pure love, purer than we could imagine love could be. Pure because impurities would come from entropy and entropy is a by-product of this universe, not eternity. He also would have to be that same pure love yesterday, today and forever because he always was and always will be.

I don't believe that God's pure love can be limited to a certain church, or a specific religion or philosophy. These are all vehicles or tools to get closer to God, but they are not God. Jesus asked us to be one with him in his body. When we think of the word "body" we usually think of body like the human body. However, body is also another word for an organization. Many churches claim to be that organization to which Jesus was referring. Jesus asked us to believe in him and be a part of the Kingdom of Heaven on Earth. God is love. His kingdom is the "domain" of God's love. His body is the living organization to which those who love him belong. So, the Kingdom of Heaven must be the Kingdom of God's love. This is where we belong. Jesus and His apostles taught that we have this kingdom within us if we love God, and our neighbor as our self. There are those who claim to know all there is to know about God, but they are fooling themselves. He is much too big for our puny human minds to comprehend. Even Jesus spoke in analogies, metaphors and parables so that people could grasp what he was saying about God. Some would argue that because they have studied the life of Jesus or the Bible they know all they need to know about the subject. Jesus is fully God but, in this universe, he also was fully human, which limited what he could say and do. God certainly can do much more than Jesus was restrained from doing in his human form. It would be like a man agreeing to be a dog for a time. He might be the best possible dog, but he still is a dog (no disrespect intended) and is limited by what dogs can and cannot do. Does calling God "pure love" put Him in too small of a box?

Certainly, he is so, so much more than *just* love, isn't He? We cannot know what pure love is because we have never seen it. It is beyond our abilities to define. Human love is passion, intimacy, friendship, commitment, and healthy relationships. It is an energy that it makes life want to emerge. It is the unity of our physical, mental and spiritual nature. It is the desire to bond: for two to become one. And pure love is the perfect version of this love. We cannot comprehend pure love until we die and experience it for ourselves in Heaven. So, saying God is pure love is not a small definition at all.

Does any individual or religion know all there is to know about God's love? How could they possibly. God is perfect, pure love. We can only sneak a glimpse of God in this lifetime of eighty years or so or even in the six-thousand-year history of civilization. As Paul said, we look at God through a mirror, a mere reflection of the true God. It will take an eternity to really get to know and understand his love and we will have to emerge on a higher level of existence (in Heaven) where we will be better equipped to understand it.

Just because God is too big to fully understand, though, doesn't mean we shouldn't try to know more about him. We should be like the child who loves her parents before knowing what love is or knowing much about her parents' life at all.

Thomas Aquinas (1225–1275) is one of the most well-known and respected theologians of all times. He wrote extensively about God and His relationship to humanity. Among many of the things he is known for is his, "Proof of God". That proof included five points: (*parenthesis added*)

1. **First Mover**—anything moved gets moved from something else (*like the golf ball sized seed that was moved by God from eternity to create the universe*)
2. **First Cause**—some things are caused, and anything caused is caused by something else (*the seed was caused by something else, God*)
3. **Necessary Being**—every contingent being at some time did not exist (*even if there is such a thing as Universal Consciousness it didn't always exist*)
4. **Greatest Being**—the greatest in truth are the greatest in being (*that is God*)
5. **Intelligent Designer**—unintelligent things act for an end that they cannot choose. They therefore must be directed by an intelligence not their own (*God again*)

Thomas Aquinas spent a lifetime writing and defending his theology attempting to define our relationship with God. His proof of God has been continuously debated through the ages. It doesn't take a genius to question it. All you need to do is simply claim the opposite:

1. **No First Mover**—the initial seed spontaneously appeared without being moved into the universal space (*it was self-created spontaneously out of nothing?*)
2. **No First Cause**—The seed appeared randomly without cause (*so everything else in the universe has a cause and an effect except it?*)
3. **No Necessary Being**—Everything and everyone is contingent or temporary or will be reincarnated (*if the same consciousness is reincarnated over and over, are you contingent or temporary? Why do people who have near death experiences see relatives? Shouldn't they be off on another incarnation?*)
4. **No Greatest Being**—all equal in truth and being, no one is greater (*of course, nobody is smarter, wiser or greater than you*)
5. **No Intelligent Designer**—Everything is just randomly doing what it was born to do without a designer (*so everything has a randomly generated, meaningless purpose? If things without purpose become extinct, why does anything exist?*)

He fought hard and wrote many, many books arguing his case. He was best known for his Summa Theologica which contained 38 treatises, 612 questions, 3,120 separate sections. It asked and answered ten thousand questions. Then, near the end of his life on December 6, 1273, while at mass, he had a vision where he was shown Heaven. When he woke up, he told his associates that he could no longer write because Heaven is beyond the comprehension of human beings and that all he had written was of little value.

> *"I can write no more... I can write no more. I have seen things which make my writings like straw."*
> —*Thomas Aquinas*

What he saw was unspeakably magnificent. He witnessed the reality of Heaven and he was astonished, amazed and humbled by it. So much so that he never wrote again.

Jesus is God and he was in this universe so if we describe him aren't we describing God's pure love? No because everything in this universe is tainted by entropy including the human side of Jesus.But the Bible says that he was without sin. Sin is only a part of entropy. We usually refer to sin as anything that offends God. Living out our natural, but entropic, lives does not offend God. It is how He set up the whole thing. When we speak of sin, we don't usually refer to other things that entropy affects like our health, things that naturally breakdown over time and how water erosion created the Grand Canyon. Jesus was affected by entropy, not sin. He suffered and died on a cross because of entropy. Pure love would not suffer or die because it has no entropy that could kill it. But God, our Father, wanted Jesus to feel our pain, suffering and our entropy. He couldn't do that unless he limited Jesus physically to being human with our "original sin" of entropy. Everything in this universe has the original sin of entropy built in to it. It is why things break down, age and die. It is why time passes. Jesus kept his entropy under control by his love and never turned his back on the Father. He broke the death spell of entropy, being the first to be raised from the dead and allowed back into Heaven to show us the way we needed to go.

Analysis of love has been going on throughout history. Plato talked about a hierarchy of love: body, soul, state and eternity. He envisioned a series of elevations from animalistic desire or lust, to friendship, to a theological vision of love. Jesus and his apostles talked about the importance of love and the different kinds of love. He taught that God is love and that we are reflections of His love. Today psychologists analyze love breaking it down into its components. First comes passion or physical desire, arousal and sexual behavior. Then comes the intimacy of friendship and lovers. Finally, there is the free will decision to love and form permanent relationships over many years. It seems so easy to define but difficult to do.

The test of genuine love is action; good intentions are not enough. Even words of love are inadequate; what counts are your actions. God's commandments are action oriented: love God and your neighbor as you love yourselves. Jesus said people who speak of love but do not live it, will not emerge in Heaven. Love in God's commandments is a verb. An action we take or a decision we make. In what may be the most famous passage on love in the New Testament, Paul defines love saying, "...Love is patient; love is kind. It is not jealous, it is not pompous, it is not inflated, it is not rude, it does not seek its own interests, it is not quick-tempered, it does not brood over injury, it does not rejoice over wrongdoing but rejoices with the truth. It bears all things, believes all things, hopes all things, endures all things." (I Cor. 13: 4-7). Every time Paul describes love he uses a verb such as "love is patient". The verb conveys an action (it doesn't seek its own interests), an occurrence (doesn't rejoice over wrongdoing) or a state of being (love is kind).

Love is the Glue that Binds Everything Together

Love holds everything in the universe together, even atoms. Everything is made of atoms and atoms consists of sub-atomic particles that have no real meaning as isolated entities but can only be understood by their actions: connections and relationships. Love is with us down to our sub-atomic components. For instance, think about what goes into the birth of a child. A man and a woman join as one beginning an amazing process. Then the man's sperm and the woman's egg unite as one composite cell that begins (through entropy) multiplying: two cells and then four, and then eight, over and over until amazingly becoming the single, fully functioning, multi-trillion celled baby human being. It is a miracle to watch a newborn cry to communicate, drink its mother's milk, grasp you with their little hands and move their tiny bodies without any special training. The process doesn't stop there. The baby grows to be a fully functioning adult replacing almost all its cells thousands of times during its lifetime. That baby doesn't do this alone. As it grows, it is helped by many loving people such as parents, grandparents, doctors, nurses, teachers, coaches and friends.

Back to the sub-atomic particles that are held together by a pattern of unity (love) allowing the bonding of atoms. Without electrons, binding to protons there would be no chemistry, no molecules, just gas. We know that atoms are 99.9% empty. That is right; the universe is made up of atoms that are 99.9% empty therefore the universe is 99.9% empty (maybe that is how it all fit in that tiny initial seed). Everything we see that looks solid is not. Atoms are patterns of probability waves that form vibrating molecules that, in turn, make up multi-dimensional, interdependent organisms like us. The whole universe is a giant energy pattern and anything solid in it is temporary. Science use to teach that the universe was like a giant machine, like a watch, with each solid thing being a part working together to keep the mechanism going. Now it tells us that the universe is more like a giant thought with no real parts just energy and probability patterns. If it is a thought, whose thought could it be? I vote God's thought.

Not everything is moving from order to disorder. There are open systems that take in energy, matter and information from outside of themselves and use them to create greater order. These open systems are living beings. Life would not exist without love. There are many examples of how cells bond to keep us alive. Such as the processing of energy into sugar to form proteins and amino acids. These help us duplicate cells, spread information and process what we need to live. Deoxyribonucleic Acid, DNA, from one living being is bonded to the DNA of another to create a new life. (it is interesting that DNA spelled backwards is AND). The natural order of things, through entropy, is for new things to get old, for things to breakdown, disintegrate and die. Love fights back by regluing the broken pieces back together. This isn't science class, so I am not going to get more technical here. Just understand that love's ability to bond is the key to life.

Our brain operates on about ten trillion connections between neurons. There are some three billion nucleotides, or bits of information connected in each person's DNA. Trillions of individual atoms and cells pulling together forming a communications network of immense processing power. Trillion of love connections!

Humans are not born knowing all they need to know. At an early age, they develop memory maps, ready-made cognitive "templates" of various kinds, that control as much as ninety-five percent of what we do. We know how to walk and talk because of memory maps. Most of our actions are done unconsciously, almost automatically, because these maps of our habits dictate much of what we do. Memory maps connect our actions, step by step and are another form of love.

Love Expands Through Emergence

Love turns disorder into order. The initial universal "seed" exploded, chaotically sending pieces in all directions. It was up to love to round them up and pull them back together. Something greater emerging out of nothing but some lesser components. This happens over-and-over in this universe: chemistry emerges from physics, biology from chemistry, psychology from neurobiology…and so on. It is how a tiny seed can create a fruit tree, a person or the entire universe. It is how a pattern is formed, a decision is made, a structure is developed, or a trend is started. It does the opposite of entropy.

Everything in nature emerges through the intentional transformation from something on a lower level to something on a higher level. For instance, take reading: letters form syllables that combine on a higher level into words, words combine on a higher level into sentences, then paragraphs, chapters, books and genres. Each level of complexity builds on the lower, simpler one. From the infinitesimal seed that started the universe 13.7 billion years ago, until now, we can see the role of emergence in action. Bacterial colonies can exhibit intelligence not found in individual bacteria. Ants, bees and even people can band together forming a synthesis on a higher level and doing more than each could do on its own level. Cells can join forming complex organisms like human beings. Are we it? Is humanity as good as it gets? Are we the end of the emergence possibilities? Why can't there be another level of emergence for humanity? I believe that with enough love, we can emerge on the next level in heaven forever.

Life appeared soon after the temperature of planet earth cooled. According to the fossil records, most animal and plant life emerged during the Cambrian Explosion about 540 million years ago. Consciousness mysteriously materialized during the Cambrian Explosion, then language without any forerunner showed up. Human beings set themselves apart from the rest of the living species. Before the Cambrian explosion, most organisms were simple, composed of individual cells. God's intervention to move things along miraculously changed our world.

An individual water molecule is not wet. Wetness comes when zillions of water molecules connect. Individual atoms have no color. Color comes from atoms joining together as molecules, each absorbing different light waves and transmitting others. A brain neuron has no thoughts. Thought emerges as millions of neurons shuttle electro-chemical impulses through ordered networks. Love bonds individuals together and *something greater emerges* but it requires a lot of love.

Life is more than the sum of its parts, it is the cascading of emergent cells. DNA provides no information unless a whole chain of nucleotides is strung together, to create information. A letter in the alphabet means very little until it is used in a word or a paragraph. Then paragraphs unite to tell a story. The entire operating system of our brains including our perceptions, thoughts, senses and emotions are components of our emergent mind. Individual plants, animals, or people transcend themselves becoming something greater such as a rain forest, a pack, a church, or a country. They form a composite oneness, maintaining their individual traits while emerging as a larger whole. This is true on all levels of the natural universe.

Love, like water, can be as small as a drop or as huge as the ocean. It could be a ray of light or a huge and brilliant star. It grows, it multiplies and spreads. It is infectious and life giving. If you pass love along to others, then you are love personified. If you love, you have God within you: a lot of love, a lot of God or a little love, a little of God.

Love is like the electromagnetic spectrum that consists of radiation of varying wavelengths from radio, to microwave, infrared, visible, ultraviolet, x-ray and gamma rays. A very small portion of the spectrum is visible to the human eye. Just as most of the electromagnetic spectrum lies outside of our perception, much of God's spectrum of light (love) is inaccessible to us. Love exists in a range from the very rudimentary bonding to the very purest form achievable in this universe. You can love God, people, ideas or things very differently but each is still a struggle for love. The concept is to bring as much of the spectrum of love into the light as possible.

First Love God with all your heart, soul and mind—with all your being

To love God means a dedication of our entire being to his will. Placing him first in our mind and heart, always speaking respectfully about Him and communicating with Him in prayer. The spirit of the Commandments demands far more than what is written. Love of God needs to happen every waking moment of the day. We need to be lifelong learners about God and His love and then live it through our actions.

Love is often described as an emotion or feeling but true love—what the New Testament writers called agape love—is not based on feelings at all. Agape love can change your life and set you free. And it all begins with a decision you make. Agape love is the decision to consider the needs of others; to give without demanding in return; and to overlook an offense or forgive an enemy. Most of all, agape love is a decision to receive and respond to God's love. All our efforts to love others will not bear fruit unless we are responding to His love. As the Bible says, "We love, because He first loved us" (1 John 4:19). God's love is more than we can comprehend. "As high as the heavens are above the earth, so high are my ways above your ways and my thoughts above your thoughts." (Isaiah 55:9). Words are inadequate or inappropriate to describe God's love. He loves because it is who He is like water is wet because of what it is. He never changes but we need to constantly change to keep moving in His direction. Our love is impure and limited because life in this universe is hampered constantly by entropy. We are made "In His Image" but like a reflection in a mirror, our likeness is imperfect and distorted. Our love tends to be conditional, self-seeking and emotional. "I will love you if you do this or that…" Agape love demands that we strive to love as Jesus loved.

> *"Probe deep within God. Explore every corner. Search every angle. Love is all you find."*
> —*Max Lucado*

Real love demands sacrifice that can't be found in self-centeredness. Sacrificial love requires that look outward and give of what we value most: our hearts, minds, souls, and strength. True love can only be understood from the actions it prompts. It also requires regular communication. How often do we pray? A real relationship takes time, effort and communication so if we want a real relationship with God we need to pray more. In Matthew 6:9, Jesus told the Apostles to "pray…in this way: (*comments in parentheses added by me*).

> *Our Father in heaven, hallowed be your name, (Oh, universal creator, dad, for all eternity, you are the holiest) your kingdom, come, your will be done, on earth as in heaven. (May your kingdom of love come to earth. Your will—keeping your commandments of love of God and self as neighbor—be done on earth as it is in heaven) Give us today our daily bread; (Meet our daily needs) and forgive us our debts, as we forgive our debtors; (Forgive us for the ways we don't love, AS we forgive those for don't love us as they should) and do not subject us to the final test but deliver us from the evil one. (Rescue us from the enemy, entropy)*

We need to learn all we can about love to defeat its natural nemesis, entropy. You may ask, why bother? In the end, entropy wins… we die and the energy and matter that make up our bodies dissipate as unworkable heat never to be useful again. Wow; wouldn't that be a depressing future? It's the one that our atheist friends expect. Others put their hope in reincarnation. They believe that they get do overs until they get it right. According to them, when their human host dies, their spirit simply animates another human body or an animal or insect. The spirit lives on to learn new lessons. There is a third option. What if our spirit can emerge on a higher level of existence? Why not? Every other living thing has done so from a single celled organism to a multi-trillion celled human being. Each level of existence has emerged from a lower level. Is a human being as good as it gets? Some argue that individual humans may merge with others and form super-human organisms much like an ant joins with other ants to form an ant colony, or bees form hives or birds flying as one in a triangle formation. I believe that God loves me and wants me to emerge and join Him in heaven.

The most important thing we can do in life is obey the two rules that Jesus outlined. Putting God first, studying His unconditional love; a love without limits, motive or judgment; and realizing that He is not dependent on our actions or achievements. There is no way that we can come close to this type of love, but we always need to strive to do better. It is like using the north star to direct your ship. We can sail off for the north star, but we won't come close to touching it. We know it is unreachable, but we strive for it anyway because it directs the way. Unconditional love, like the north star, is also unattainable in this lifetime, but seeing His way guides ours.

Love expands in ever widening circles around us. First you love your parents, then siblings, friends, spouses, children and grandchildren in ever cascading circles of love as you age. You might feel a different type of love for each. You don't continuously divide your love so that you can love more. It is not like you have a personal love account and each time a new love enters your life you make another withdrawal from it. Love multiplies, it doesn't divide. Your love expands to include each new person or thing you choose to love. Love bonds two things together as one without ceasing to be itself. It nourishes without being consumed.

"A candle that lights another candle loses nothing."
—Anonymous

Next Love Yourself

What does it mean to love ourselves? We are not talking about being selfish, self-centered or self-absorbed. We are talking about true love of our physical, mental and spiritual self. The kind of love that is in the image of God's love. Discover who you are, where you came from and what you are here to do. Appreciate the blessings and opportunities you were given and the love that gives you the confidence to serve God and others.

Do you really understand the difference between loving yourself in an honorable way and, on the other hand, being selfish and inwardly focused? Does your life reflect this understanding? How well do you love yourself? How do you demonstrate that love? Is it a struggle to rediscover and maintain your uniqueness? Do you realize and appreciate the fact that you will be the only you to ever live upon this earth; that when you die so will all your fantastic possibilities; all your gifts? Your life has a unique role that only you can fulfill. Nobody else in the world can do what you were born to do exactly the way you can do it.

You were created as the only you there will ever be. You are bombarded by people telling you that you must discover your purpose and fulfill it. You know your purpose, so you don't need another purpose. What you need to discover is how you will advance the cause of love through your actions. Your unique and special way of loving God and your neighbor as yourself. This is your mission, not your purpose.

People say they are searching for their life's purpose, but their purpose is known, and it is clear: become one with God for all eternity. What they really want to know is their mission. Their mission is their personal action plan to help fulfill humanity's purpose. It is the way they help people love God, neighbor and self, more effectively. There is one purpose but many missions. God has given you a specific mission that only you can accomplish. It will advance the cause of love in the world. You must be convinced that you have been chosen to carry out your mission.

"No one has been given your lines...the Author of the human drama entrusted your part to you alone."
—Cure For The Common Life, page 34

Loving yourself means deciding to accept love as well as give it. If you don't breathe in, you won't be able to breathe out. It is a constant flow, in and out, back and forth, ...we receive, give, then receive again. Only when you have it can you give it. All you can give is what you have been given. This is the value exchange we discussed earlier.

One important way to show love for ourselves is to respect our bodies by doing what is good for our health and well-being. Eating the right food and in the right proportion shows that we appreciate our physical health. Physical exercise increases our physical strength and endurance and invigorates our mind. It is a great way to learn discipline getting enough rest and peace. We need to use wisdom in eating, exercising, sleeping, and practicing general good healthy habits.

If we really love and respect ourselves, the second thing to do is try everything to protect ourselves from the influences of the world (entropy) that would defile our body, mind and spirit. Knowing that we are children of God should help us make worthy choices of actions and our companions. This doesn't mean that we wall ourselves off from everyone that we judge to not be acting in a loving way. Maybe they don't know how to love, and our role is to help them learn. There is a difference between recognizing and guarding against entropy's influence over us and reaching out to help those that are in its clutches and helping them find their way. Understanding entropy and recognizing it when it rears its ugly head is an important way to love ourselves.

The third thing we can do to develop love for ourselves is to appreciate who we are. When we love ourselves, we recognize that

God knows we are one-of-a-kind, and he has given us special gifts. We are each unique. We were created in His Image, so if we love God how can we not love our self and others? It is so important that we do not compare ourselves to others but rather work to appreciate and develop who we are individually. Typically, self-assessments are in comparison to others or to some ideal or standard. Instead, compare yourself to who you were yesterday not to how you compare to everyone else around you. There is only one person that will laugh at all your jokes, have the same taste as you, or think about things exactly the way you will, and that person is you. Focus on improving yourself versus yourself, not versus others.

As they say, it is never too late to be who we are meant to be. Set goals, work hard, be patient, and believe that you can do it if you have the courage to press on. Remembering your purpose and your mission, and when you understand your potential; act. You will have the boldness to try new things and discover new talents. Hard work is the only way to learn and grow, but it is important to balance that with good, healthy fun; don't take yourself too seriously. Laugh whenever you can and feel your joy. Loving yourself involves the discovery of the true wonder of you: the present you and the many possibilities of you. Realizing you are irreplaceable; like no other.

> *"Alas for those that never sing. But die with all their music within them."*
> —Oliver Wendell Holmes

The fourth way we love ourselves is to forgive ourselves. If we truly love ourselves, we will recognize that when we make mistakes, we can turn to God or those we hurt and ask for forgiveness. As Jesus taught us in the Our Father, "forgive us our trespasses *as* we forgive others". There is that "as" word again. He will forgive us *as much as* we are willing to forgive others. He will help us to turn our lives around and have the strength to get back on the right path. He loves us and will forgive us if we sincerely mean to change our lives. He will help us forgive ourselves and regain our self-respect and self-worth. Forgiving ourselves means accepting our physical appearance; our level of mental sharpness; our personality quirks and our sense of humor (or lack of it). Evaluate how much you care about others and how you can improve. Reflect but don't dwell on your faults, flaws and shortcomings. Learn from them and move on noting what is good and decent about yourself and not feeding the negative thoughts. Embrace your whole self; love your whole package unconditionally.

When you forgive someone, you are telling yourself that you do not want to waste any more time or energy on this person or event. You need to give up your destructive thoughts about the situation and believe that life will be better when you stop thinking about it.

Refusing to forgive by holding onto the anger, resentment and the sense of betrayal will make you miserable. You will remain bitter and angry and the person or event that caused it continues to make you the victim. Forgiving the offense doesn't mean forgetting it or that you condone it. It just means that it isn't worth thinking about any more. When you forgive, you do it for yourself. The hurts won't heal until you forgive. It is not possible to be present and available for a new relationship until you heal the hurt and upsets of the past. You can never live in the present and create a new and exciting future if you are stuck in the past. Let go, move on and stay positive.

One of the ways that entropy fights the love you have for yourself is through shame. Shame robs you of God's blessings and it tries to rule you, so you won't feel worthy of God's love. It is an entropic downward spiral: sin (entropy) leads to guilt, guilt to shame, shame to condemnation and death. Instead of emerging, you are submerging. This is entropy in action. Sin is something you do (action), guilt is something you feel (information) and shame is something you carry (spirit). The weight of shame drags you down, overtakes your spirit and condemnation takes you out. Don't be ruled by the shame, judgment, opinions and attitudes of others. God specifically tells us not to do this, so those who do it are not God's favorites but ones who are disobeying God. Don't feel less because of them. Feel sorry for them and pray that God shows them the error of their ways. Don't let past weaknesses drag you down. Learn from your mistakes, become a better person and then move on. Embrace the present and realize that you can't change the past. Move forward with courage, faith and hope. Jesus said he is the judge, not other people. Since God's mind is so much greater than any person's, I will trust Jesus to judge me, not other small-minded human beings. He knows better than anyone else what the true circumstances were surrounding the event you are ashamed of.

Being ashamed of past actions can lead to depression. Fortunately, God's love is the definite cure for depression. Entropy is the reason for twisted thoughts and distorted emotions and they fade in the presence of God's love. Entropy cannot control or rule you when your heart and mind are full of God's love. Ideally, we would push all entropic thoughts and behaviors out of our life on our own but, many times, we need the help from a friend or a counsellor or even medication to change our thought processes. As we love ourselves the way God desires, we are prepared to truly love others. Self-love and a love of God is the foundation upon which a life of love and service to others is based. If we need help to make this happen, we need to accept the help.

Finally, Love Your Neighbor as Yourself

One way that we demonstrate our love for God is by loving His children. Since God is the Father of this universe, all human beings are His children (not just the good ones). The basic nature of God is love. When we love others with unselfish love, we are showing our love for God. We are commanded to love God and love our neighbor as our self. Jesus gave us guidance on how to love others in the Sermon on the Mount. He encouraged us to interior purity and spiritual transformation urging us to:

- Avoid murder by not getting angry
- Avoid adultery by not lusting
- Instead of making oaths, tell the truth
- Don't retaliate, forgive
- Love your enemies, be a peacemaker
- Do good to those who can't help you

- Stop judging (that is His job)
- Do God's will—love

Everyone who is not me, is my neighbor. My family, friends, associates, enemies and those I have not met yet—are all my neighbors because they are all God's children. We demonstrate our love for them by nurturing feelings of tolerance, patience, kindness, helpfulness, and compassion in our hearts as well as in our actions accepting and loving them all, no matter who they are or where they live. We strive to not be negative, judgmental or angry towards our brothers and sisters. We try to understand rather than judge and condemn. We accept differences as strengths and we learn from each other.

Loving others means being there for them in their joy, happiness, and triumphs but also in their anger, disappointments and sadness. If you want a relationship, focus on what you love about others, don't judge them and tell them how they should change their lives. Relationships are deepened by generous acts between giver and receiver. As your love grows; you and everyone around you benefits. Care feels good and helps those that are suffering.

Americans have always believed in community service (faith and works). People gather and help each other in churches and synagogues, Rotary Clubs, soup kitchens and political meetings. By participating in such groups, we can really change the lives of others or just make someone feel better because paid attention to them. Our love for God will never be judged by our words alone. It will be based on our actions and those actions must come from within. Love for God, for ourselves, and others should become our motivation to act.

Love compels us to give so that we alleviate the pain and suffering of others. Instead of just seeking to fulfill our emotional and physical needs (receiving), we give of ourselves. God doesn't love us for who we are but because of *who He is*. Likewise, we should love others because of who *we are*; and not because of who they are or what they say or do. That means tolerating their faults and weaknesses and appreciating their kindness. Jesus told us to love our enemies including people who intentionally hurt or humiliate us, who we disagree with, who we don't understand and who are wrong. To love them means we must help them. It is easy to love the people who are lovable but to love our enemies is difficult.

Growing in love and relationships is the way to overcome the ill effects of entropy. We are reminded constantly of the price we will pay if we don't push for more love. Cancer cells are an example of what happens when a cell stops seeking relationships with the neighboring cells. Instead of cooperating and integrating, the cell becomes disentangled, autonomous and separate. They serve their own interest and do nothing to help the cells around them. The cancer cell hoards the blood supply, oxygen and nutrients that it normally would pass along to its neighbors. It multiplies into a group of rebel cells that live for themselves and selfishly reproduce until they eventually kill their human host and themselves. Sounds like what is happening with our civilization today.

In other words, love or be consumed by entropy. Entropy will kill you while love brings life. The end of Deuteronomy summarizes life's choice: life or death and destruction (or you can say: love or entropy). Karen Armstrong, an accomplished religious author, said that you can't learn to dance, drive, play an instrument or cook by simply reading about them in a book. The book can provide important background information, but you need to experience it for yourself: to live it. To love others as ourselves, we can't just read about it, we must experience it by serving others, showing kindness, sacrificing, building meaningful relationships, being generous, making associations, forming bonds, cooperating, forgiving and being there for our family, friends and others. Reading about all these things without doing them is meaningless.

Even animals exhibit a primitive form of love. Animals, like people, have an instinct to pass their genes on to the next generation. Some believe it is the primary reason that parents care for their children. They want to insure they stay alive long enough to pass on the family genes. I hope my parents love me for more than my genes. This approach makes love seem like simply the mechanism of biological transmission, but it is much more than that.

Besides biological transmission of genes, there is cultural transmission; the selective communication of ideas, beliefs, memories, habits, rituals and technology. Since the beginning of civilization, humans have formed small groups to share food and protect themselves against the elements, wild animals and other people who may want to harm them. People formed mutually beneficial relationships with others they trusted and counted on for support. In these groups, they created a culture allowing one generation to pass its ideas, wisdom and dreams on to the next.

Cultural transmission is facilitated by language which is one of the biggest differences between human beings and other mammals. We can create new things or destroy them with our words. We can learn from the words uttered in the past and teach others how to live purposeful, loving lives with our words. Words help us define our reality.

Entropy undermines love wherever it sprouts up. Through fundamentalism and infighting over tenants of the faith, schisms, splintering denominations and all forms of religious persecution, we are falling out of love with God and entropy is winning. With rising depression, addiction, obesity and mental illness we are falling out of love with ourselves and entropy is gaining. With crimes using knives and guns, terrorist attacks, racism and economic rivalries we are falling out of love with our neighbors and, again, entropy is gaining on us. It is eroding away our love connections, watering them down, and breaking the bonds that hold us together. We need to push for greater connectivity to reverse the devastating consequences of entropy. That means getting away from all those things that separate us and coming together as one.

> "Bless those who persecute you; bless and do not curse them. Rejoice with those who rejoice, weep with those who weep. Have the same regard for one another; do not be haughty but associate with the lowly; Do not be wise in your own estimation. do not repay evil for evil; be concerned for what is noble in the sight of all. If possible, on your part, live at peace with all.
>
> (Rom 12: 14-18)

Jesus came to cleanse and heal us of entropy (sin) so that we would be better prepared to love the Father in Heaven and each other here on earth. Jesus, as a human, struck his first major blow against entropy when He outsmarted Satan in the desert at the beginning of His public ministry, and continued to fight the forces of entropy throughout the remainder of his human life by curing the sick, raising the dead, multiplying the loaves and fishes, walking on water, dying for us at Calvary and then defeating entropy by rising from the dead. He showed us that entropy doesn't have to control us.

Jesus said, "I am the way, and the truth, and the life; no one comes to the Father but through me." (John 14:6). Because of this Biblical passage, many believe that, unless you become a Christian, you will not be allowed into Heaven. However, if Jesus is the physical manifestation of the Father and the Father is love, shouldn't anyone with enough love be acceptable to the Father? Being a Christian helps us learn more about how to love but, I don't believe that it is the only way we learn about love. I believe that when we die, we face Jesus first before entering Heaven. It is in that moment He will judge if we gained enough love in our lifetime to pass into Heaven. As the judge *of* our love, he is *the way, the truth and the life* that leads to the Father in Heaven. While on earth, under the influence of entropy, we are more than capable of acting against our better judgment. So, besides expressing love with our actions, we need to ask God for the grace to carry out what we desire. Grace is unmerited favor or kindness from God. It makes everything possible because it comes from the creator of everything. Humans are fragile and weak. We need supernatural medicine to fight off the disease of entropy. Its power and forces are too great without an injection of grace. It is divine assistance that regenerates us and helps us live in an upright way. We can live beyond our circumstances, problems, troubles and weaknesses if we believe that God will strengthen us when we ask. Grace is trust in God's energy instead of our own. It is sad when someone needs help and is too proud to ask. They insist that they will overcome any of life's obstacles on their own without anyone's help. These people ultimately fail. They may look like a success on the outside, but they cannot possibly amass enough love on their own to defeat entropy.

There are many angry people who do not understand the concept of grace. They claim that God decides who gets it and who doesn't. In other words, God plays favorites. He decides who will get enough love to move on to Heaven and who will not. But God is more like the sun shining equally on all. If you stay in the sunlight, you will always enjoy its benefits; if you choose to go into the shade, you will block yourself from the sun and all its many advantages. God's love is always available to everyone except those who choose to remain in the shade (in sin; in entropy). "There but by the grace of God go I…?" People say this when they see poverty, sickness, crime and other unpleasant things in life. They tell themselves that if God had not blessed them with His grace, they too might have such a wretched life. Or they think that those things just happen to people who do not do what God wants them to do. Since Roe versus Wade did over 60 million aborted babies in the United States die because God didn't want them to live? They never got the chance to choose love. Their parents made a wrong choice but I'm sure God them all into heaven. How about all those poor physically or mentally afflicted people in their wretched situations? Doesn't God care about them? Of course, he does. They are where they are because of decisions they have made or because of their life circumstances planting or taking them there. What happens next is up to them and up to us. We need to help them because they are our neighbors. We need to love them as we love ourselves which means helping them have better lives even as we seek better lives for ourselves. And, most importantly, we need to be there for them without judging them. We are not living their lives in their circumstances, so it isn't our place to pass judgment on them. God clearly stated that judgment belongs to him and him alone.

God has been working throughout history, caring for humanity, leading and helping to protect us. Jesus was God's personal entry into our history, teaching, healing, gathering and being the perfect role model to lead us all to heaven. God desires to work for us and in us where we are. Jesus gave us the good news that, although we all are sinners, we are reconciled with God. All we need to do is remain in His love.

God's presence in our hearts brings the opposite of self-indulgence. "In contrast, the fruit of the Spirit is love, joy, peace, patience, kindness, generosity, faithfulness, gentleness, self-control." (Gal 5:22, 23). God's love is not static or self-centered; it reaches out and draws us in. God sets the pattern of true love, the basis for all love relationships--when you love someone profoundly; you are willing to pay profoundly for that person's love. Jesus paid the ultimate price for our love and then offered us the new life that he gained for us. Our love must be like Jesus'. We must be willing to give up our own comfort, security and sometimes our lives so that others might join us in receiving God's love. Because he emerged from death to new life, he cleared the path for us to do the same.

Empedocles (493–433 BC) was a Greek philosopher who taught that the universe is composed of fire, air, water, and earth, which mingle and separate under the influence of the opposing principles of Love and Strife. Strife is discord, fighting, dissention which is the opposite of synchronization, coordination and coherence. He was on the right track. His strife is a partial description of entropy. It is love and entropy that are the opposing forces influencing reality.

In the story of the Garden of Eden there are two trees. One tree is called the Tree of Life and if Adam and Eve ate the fruit of that tree they would live forever in peace and love. The other tree is called the Tree of Knowledge of Good and Evil. If they ate from that tree they would know the difference between good and evil, would have no peace in their life time and would die. I think this story lays out the two primal forces of existence. The Tree of Life is really the Tree of Love and partaking of it leads to eternal life. The Tree of Knowledge of Good and Evil is the Tree of Free Will to choose love or entropy. We are born as a part of this tree but hope to be graphed onto the Tree of Life one day.

The most important thing we can do in life is obey the two commandments that Jesus outlined. Putting God first, studying His unconditional love; a love without limits, motive or judgment. There is no way that we can come close to God's unconditional love, but we need to strive to always do better. Next, we must discover the true wonder of who we are; why we are so special, unique and lovable.

Finally, we need to learn to love others "as" we love ourselves. If we don't love ourselves very much, we won't have much love to give to others.

> *"Think of a cross-section of a tree. Each ring represents not a replacement of the previous ring, not a rejection of them, but an embracing of them, a comprising of them, and inclusion of them in something bigger. The tree's previous growth is integrated into, and in fact, is essential to, the tree's continuing growth and strength."*
> —Generous Orthodoxy, page 315

Humanity needs to look at life the same way. Every day builds on the day before. We don't replace the activities of yesterday with the activities of today. We don't replace the people we interact with yesterday with the people we interact with today. We embrace them and include them in our ever-emerging life. They all add to our continuing growth, strength and multiplying love.

CHAPTER 4

Love's Battle Plan

"The deepest desire of our hearts is for union with God. God created us for union with himself. This is the original (and I would add, only valid) purpose of our lives."

—Brennan Manning

The Bible prophesizes a final battle between the forces of God and the forces of Satan, called the Battle of Armageddon (Rev 19:11–16, 19–21). Throughout history people have claimed the coming of this battle as a foreshadowing of the end of the world. They say it will take place on the fields of Megiddo, Israel where all the major powers of the world will clash. I have been there. It is a wide-open field as far as you can see. A great place for an old fashion battle but not the way wars are fought today. Anyway, I don't think we need to wait for the battle to start because it has been raging since the beginning of time. The two warring factions are love (God) and entropy (Satan) and they have been fighting since the Big Bang. By our actions, we volunteer for one army or the other.

To prepare to fight we need to study the enemy's motives, strategies, tactics, actions and resources as well as our own. Then we need to train for how to attack and neutralize the enemy.

- Entropy's mission is to block the emergence of life at every level of existence. It will attack all forms of the living from the smallest to the largest. It tries to stop sub-atomic particles from bonding together, destroys cells and tissues, tears living beings apart through cancer, disease and aging. Its purpose is to stop humanity from emerging on its next level in Heaven. Entropy wants to convert all the universe's energy into useless heat as soon as possible to end all emergences.
- Life (love) stands in its way. The living fights off entropy through love: bonding, uniting and joining forces to push back against entropy.

Think of the battle between love/entropy like you do the ancient Chinese concept of Yin/Yang. The Chinese view the two as a dynamic balance of opposites. As the world ceaselessly changes, it constantly readjusts the balance of Yin and Yang. The two forces are interdependent; both forces need each other. They blend together into one seamless whole. The ratio Yin/Yang is a metaphor for the ratio of love/entropy. Because God created the universe for mankind to make a choice between love and entropy, both forces are necessary and are interdependent. Unlike Yin/Yang, the goal is not to harmonize the two but to have one (love) overpower the other (entropy) on a spiritual level allowing the souls of the living to emerge in Heaven for all eternity.

Since there are only two primal forces at work, love and entropy, and they are interdependent, your spirit must constantly keep filling itself with one or the other. They are complimentary opposites, and each defines the other. Picture the Yin/Yang symbol and substitute love (white) and entropy (black) for the two primary parts of it. Think of each as a fluid that will not mix with the other fluid. If you pour in one it will force the other out. For instance, pour in the love fluid so that the entropy fluid gets forced out.

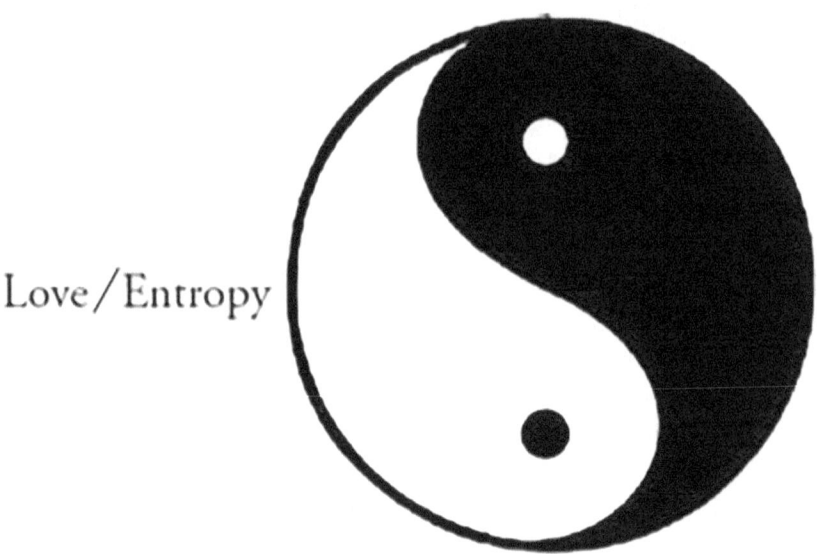

Love/Entropy

There is a constant struggle with love wanting to overcome your natural tendency to be filled with entropy. On your physical level, entropy wins in the end and your body dies and dissipates as heat. This was always the natural path since the day you were born. But not true when it comes to your spirit. It does not have to surrender to entropy. Love can seize control your spirit and with enough love, you can burst through the universal border into Heaven.

So then how does love win, in the end? Every individual has a love force around them and the strength of the field is proportionate to the amount of love you possess. So, if you possess a lot of love, you will give off a strong love force that will, like gravity, attract others. God is pure love and he is everywhere, but primarily outside of this universe (because eternity is much larger than this universe). If you have enough love and are close enough to God, he will, like gravity, pull you towards him. The boundary of the universe will not be strong enough to hold your spirit from passing over.

Where do the troops of the love army train?

It seems obvious that the church should be the primary place one would go to prepare for battling entropy. After all, church is the place we are supposed to learn about loving God, our neighbors and our self, isn't it? If it is, then the 96 percent of the 7 billion people in the world who claim to believe in God, should make love's army an overwhelming force. The problem is that entropy has sent undercover agents into the churches for centuries. It has subverted many of the people of God, turning them against each other. It is behind the thousands of splinter groups of God-fearing people. It has caused division, anger and even hate between different church groups. How does this happen? As a training tool to see how entropy destabilized the church's message of love, let's look closer at one church group, Jesus Christ's Christian Church.

Shalom

The early Christian Church met in houses and followed the lead of a handful of Apostles and disciples. Non-Christians would marvel at how they loved one another. Originally, the church was simply known as "Shalom" or "peace" In Hebrew, the word means wholeness, a full, harmonious, joyful life: a life that is physically, mentally and spiritually balanced.

> *"Shalom is understood to mean peace, but peace is only a part of the word's real meaning. The root word Shalem means completeness."*
> —Celso Cukierkorn

Members of the early Christian Church believed that they were called to bring a "peaceful attitude" to all people. After Jesus was resurrected, he greeted the Apostles with the word, "Peace". Mary always talked about peace in her apparitions. The Apostles preached that the Kingdom of God, as Mark's gospel called it, or the Kingdom of Heaven, Matthew's term, will come to the earth. That meant that the

Kingdom of Love would one day rule the world. Let's pray that day comes but it is difficult to see it from here.

> *"Peace I leave you…my own peace I give you. Not as the world gives do I give it to you. Do not let your hearts be troubled, neither let them be afraid. Stop allowing yourselves to be agitated and disturbed: and do not permit yourselves to be fearful and intimidated and unsettled."*
>
> *(John 14:27)*

Jesus said that His peace was different than the peace that the world offers. If we possess His peace we have no reason to fear, worry, be anxious or stressed out. To have His peace, we need to trust Him and do what He asks us to do: love. Worry, fear and dread rob you of your peace. Have faith that God is in control and love courageously.

Peace is about going with the flow, not resisting but resting in the knowledge that "God's got this." Peace means being content, quiet and calm regardless of our circumstances: letting go and letting God handle it. It is not always about being sure how something will turn out but sure that it will be as God intended. Patiently knowing that, "this too shall pass". Nothing stays the same for long. Every life has ups and downs. God really wants you to share in his peace.

Christianity is not the only religion preaching peace. Islam is known as a religion of peace. Om Shanti, Shanti, Shanthi is the emphatic Hindu Vedic blessing of peace. The absolute emphasis on compassion and ahimsa in Buddhism and Jainism is about peace.

God's peace happens when the world cries out in a panic upset, agitated, disturbed, fearful, intimidated or unsettled. If we react calmly and with Christ's peace, others will see this and want to join forces with us. We need to trust God to help us make the right choices in our lives. We can't go through life blaming others for what happens. Whatever happens teaches us and makes us more loving. So, when the world tells you to be very, very afraid, God says:

> *"Be not afraid" is the most frequently repeated admonition in the Hebrew scriptures...appearing more than a hundred times from Genesis to Exodus to Psalms to Isaiah to Jeremiah."*
> —Christ Actually

The early church grew so rapidly that the Romans viewed it as a threat and tried to squash it before it swept through the empire. Putting Jesus to the most humiliating and painful public death didn't scare them off so they brutally killed all of the Apostles except John and many of the followers who put their faith into action by going out into the world to share their message of love and peace. The deaths were horrendous including crucifixions, stoning, stabbings and beheadings. This drove the followers of Jesus Christ underground where they met in secret out of fear of Roman persecution. Their secret meetings helped them become very close friends that loved each other. A major turning point in the early church occurred when the Roman Emperor Constantine converted to Christianity in 312AD. Historians still debate whether Constantine's conversion was sincere or politically motivated. Some say he converted because of his success on the battlefield using the Christian Cross. He looked up to the sky before a major battle and saw a cross with the words "*with this conquer*". He had all his soldiers put a cross on their shields and they won the battle. Others say he continued to believe in paganism but said he favored the Christian God for political unity's sake. Whatever his true motivation, it marked the end of persecution of Christians and the beginning of Christendom. In 313, Constantine issued the "Edict of Milan," which granted official tolerance of Christianity and other religions. He ordered that Sunday be granted the same legal rights as pagan feasts and that feasts in memory of Christian martyrs be recognized. Constantine's program was one of toleration only, and he continued to support both Christianity and paganism. Christianity didn't become the official religion of the empire until 380AD with a decree of Emperor Theodosius.

After Constantine declared "tolerance" of Christianity, he turned over many large public buildings to the church. Church services went from small, intimate gatherings in homes to large, dramatic theatrical productions. To make the people feel a part of it, colorful garments and high hats, large banners and group rituals were developed. Church leadership became bogged down in theatre and bureaucracy. Entropy was winning through misdirection. Church leaders got distracted from the mission of the church.

It was the invention of the Gutenberg Printing Press in 1439 that changed the Christian church forever. It played a key role in the Renaissance, Enlightenment, the Scientific Revolution and had a profound effect on the Protestant Reformation. Bibles could now be mass produced and distributed to the multitudes for the first time. In 1517, there was a major church split when Martin Luther, a Catholic priest, posted his 95 Theses or Disputation on the Power of Indulgences on the church door. It was a list of discussion topics that Martin Luther nailed to the door of Wittenberg Castle church to protest the sale of indulgences. His protest ignited the Protestant Reformation. Luther was unintentionally posting the Protestants' Declaration of Independence (a major victory for entropy). From then on, many Catholics became convinced that they should not follow the hierarchy of the church, just their own Biblical interpretations. Luther thought that the Bible should be the only authority. He didn't realize how much he was helping entropy invade the church.

Approximately eighty-five percent of communication is non-verbal such as tone, emphasis, mood, sarcasm, empathy and other attributes that cannot be translated effectively into the written words. As the printed bibles replaced the oral preaching and teaching, the information provided became depersonalized, fixed and less flexible than truth relayed personally from master to pupil (the same is happening today with text messaging on cell phones). Similar written words without the proper emphasis can mean something very different. For instance, take the sentence, "I did not say that he stole the money." Then say the sentence out loud emphasizing each word. The first time you would say, "**I** did not say…" so it could mean that someone else said it. The second time you say, "I **did not** say that… I never said it. The third time you say, "I did not say that **he** stole… I meant someone else stole it. You get the idea. Each time you emphasize a different word you dramatically change the meaning of the sentence. So, relying on written words alone can be a problem. Deceptive and manipulative preachers could take a passage from the scriptures and, by changing the emphasis or context, make it mean the opposite of what it was intended to mean.

> *"Both read the Bible day and night. But they read black while I read white."*
> —William Blake

Jesus spoke in Aramaic, his native language. After He returned to Heaven, for some seventy or more years, the gospel stories were handed down by word of mouth. Then, over the next few hundred years, they were translated and written down in the koine language, Greek common vernacular (now dead). Then it was translated into the Greek we know today, then Latin and other languages and finally into English. Do you think, along the way, something might have been lost in translation?

Saying that the only way to believe in God is to follow the Bible is very limiting. Besides, it is pretentious of us to think that we could capture all there is to know about God in a single book (putting God in a tiny box). The words are inspired by God and offers a lot of good information, but the Bible cannot tell us *all* we need to know about loving God, our neighbors and our self. We should study Holy Scriptures as part of our preparation for battling entropy but not limit ourselves to just looking there for all our answers. It is like going into battle with only one weapon.

Relying solely on "Sacred Scriptures" and claiming your interpretation is the only reliable one can be dangerous and lead you or others astray. The scriptures are inspired by God and, certainly, useful for teaching love and pointing out what needs to be done to correct entropic ways but it cannot and does not include all there is to know about God or love. Jesus did not write additional scriptures or even write things down. He probably thought that his written words would be static, unchanging, lifeless, misunderstood and misinterpreted. He did quote from scripture but often said "you have heard it said...well I say..." In other words, he did not necessarily take the scripture words literally or say that they could never be replaced by a deeper understanding as civilization progressed and matured.

> *Jesus says, "You have heard that it was said, 'You shall love your neighbor and hate your enemy.' But I say to you, 'love your enemies and pray for those who persecute you.'"*
>
> *(Matt. 5: 43,44)*

Instead of "an eye for an eye", Jesus said when your enemy strikes one cheek, turn and give him the other. This was a radical departure from the Old Testament writings. It was not the only time he changed the Old Testament passages. He knew that civilization was maturing and was ready for a more mature approach to life. The Old Testament was geared to a civilization that was in its infancy. Children need a lot of rules, laws and direction on how to live. As children grow they learn about love and how to live as adults, choosing which rules best suit them. He preached love of all people. He knew that entropy would take advantage of the "eye for an eye" idea and use it to pit one against another in all situations. "Road rage" is an "eye for an eye" example.

Scriptures can explain why we are here but when it claims to have the final word on scientific questions it often falls short. Many people have lost faith because of the preachers who insist that the Earth was created six thousand years ago, in six 24-hour days (a man-made construct), that people and dinosaurs roamed the Earth together and other such claims. Religions that claim to have all the truth cannot explain much of the reality around us. They stake their claims on faith but that doesn't square with the reality that has been uncovered over the years. Some religious people want to believe every word of the Bible *literally* despite very convincing evidence to the contrary. By insisting every word is literal and true, they cause people of little faith to turn away and those with no faith to stay away. Consider these contradictions in the order of creation:

BIBLE SCIENCE

*The Earth came before the sun and stars	*The stars and sun came before the Earth
*The Earth initially was covered by water	*Earth was a molten blob initially
*Ocean first, then dry land	*Land came first, then ocean
*Life Created on the land	*Life began in the ocean
*Plants created before the sun	*Plants developed because of the sunlight
*Land animals created after the birds	*Land animals evolved before the birds

The Bible was never intended to be a science textbook. However, just because it is inaccurate on a few scientific facts, doesn't mean that its extremely valuable religious and moral information is untrue. Today there are those who point out the scientific errors as a reason to discount the message of the entire book. Religious leaders attempted to reduce the uncertainty of life and faith in God by sticking only to what was written in the bible. They should focus on their strengths: building relationships, defining life's purpose, teaching respect, empathy and especially love. These are the areas where religion is superior to science, but science is superior to religion in defining the physical reality of the universe. We need both perspectives to understand our total reality (like the two hemispheres of our brain).

God created the universe. Over time, it has unfolded according to His plan. It was formed in "seven days" but seven of God's "days" not as we humans track our days. The Bible says that to God "one day is like a thousand years and a thousand years like one day" (2 Pet. 3:8), which, at that time that was written, was a tremendously huge, almost an incomprehensible number. We would say "one day is like a billion years and a billion years is like a day." God could take billions of human years to accomplish the creation of the universe and no time would pass in Heaven (time is an element of this universe, not eternity). The word "day" used in Genesis 1:1-5 is the Hebrew word "yom" which refers to a time period with a beginning and an end. He is behind the evolution of life from single cells to tiny viruses and bacteria to complex, multi-trillion celled humans. I can believe in religion and in science and believe that they are both just partial pictures of reality.

Words are only approximate maps of reality. In all languages, words can have more than one meaning, so reading involves making choices, understanding context, intent and local customs. Language can be misleading, ambiguous, and only selectively heard. Metaphors, analogies and parables can lead to different understanding like how two people can view the same artwork and see different things. Try describing the color of blue to a blind person. You need to see blue to understand what it looks like because color is more than the words that describe it. The written word needs human interpretation.

The Sacred Scriptures provide information that reinforces the religion it represents. The problem is that information can change its meaning over time. The Bible is a collection of 66 distinctive books written down by more than 40 different authors over 1500 years on three continents in Hebrew, Aramaic and Greek. It has been translated into hundreds of languages throughout the centuries. It has various literary genres; some texts are allegorical, some literal and some are morality stories. It can mean different things to different people. So, it has an objective and a subjective meaning that can easily be manipulated or misdirected. In other words, it is a place where entropy can run wild.

Almost ninety percent of the seven billion people in the world say they believe in God but, according to one estimate, they belong to over 14,000 religions (another source says there are over 100,000). Many claim an exclusive relationship with God and unless you join their group you will be locked out of Heaven. Religion is supposed to be a set of beliefs that explain what life is all about, who we are and how we should spend our time. It is a means to an end not the end itself. Imagine what a world it would be if the churches got together teaching love and peace and sharing what each knows about it. Instead entropy is causing more and more divisions, denominations, radical groups and individual fanatics.

One minister told me that he would never be ecumenical because he got most of his members from other churches. He wanted to put people in his pews more than he wanted to teach them about love. He preached that the "neighbors" that his members were to love were the people in the pews next to them, not those o3utside the church. These are the people who have their names written in the "Book of Life" and are "saved" so they are the ones God commanded us to care for and the rest should be converted, pitied, prayed for or forgotten (even our mothers, fathers, sisters and brothers). If I can be saved before I die, why keep living? My purpose is to spend eternity in Heaven with God and these churches say I can be saved and guaranteed a place at the great banquet in Heaven by just saying I'm sorry and I believe in God. So then, if I'm saved, I should die now and move on to Heaven, right? But if that was my attitude who would be left behind to fight the forces of entropy? Who would train the forces of love to defeat the enemy?

Too many of those who claim to be "saved" or "born again" or "spirit-filled" are hypocrites that are judgmental, condescending, unloving know-it-alls that are anything but filled with God's love. My sister died when she was 49 years old and I was heartbroken. A "minister" approached me at the wake and, before saying anything consoling, said, "Did she know the Lord?" Does that sound like a loving comment to you? If you are full of God's love, you will show compassion as an expression of that love.

In the Bible "save" means "rescue" or "heal". It does not mean automatically "saved from Hell" or rewarded eternal life without effort. It had more to do with getting out of trouble like when you are sick, oppressed, poor, imprisoned or in danger. Ironically many of the groups claiming a guaranteed place in Heaven are not much different than those who sold indulgences. I wonder what Martin Luther would say to them if he were around today. Instead of worrying about "being saved" we should be worried about loving more right now and battling entropy right where we are.

The Church should be a living body that changes when necessary: not a lifeless, rigid, formula-based business. It should be about more than escaping Hell. Members are expected to perform a certain way or get excommunicated. There is nothing wrong with holding members accountable for specific beliefs and practices while still loving and respecting them. How is throwing them out of the assembly showing them God's love? There is a place for discipline and a place for mercy. Jesus shared his last meal with the "friend" that he knew betrayed him. There doesn't have to be just one church of God's love. Saying there should be one worldwide way of participating in church is like saying there is only one way to raise your children no matter where you live in the world and under what circumstances you find yourself. Or that there should be just one type of music or art or food that satisfies all our desires and is good for us. There are many different churches in which people want to belong. The Hindu Bhagavad Gita, the Buddhist's Dhanapala, Islam's Koran, Christianity's Bible and Taoism's Tao Ching all tell people to, "Love God, practice kindness and compassion to others and strive to eliminate selfishness." Just like there are many items on a restaurant menu to satisfy your hunger, there can be different places to satisfy your hunger for God's love. When asked about people of different religions Jesus simply answered, "Those who are not against us, are for us." (Luke 9:49, 50) In other words, "Those who are not against God's love, are for it." We are all divine siblings, not because of what we believe but because we have the same Father. Hindus say honor all seekers of the truth. Know that different people require different ways of relating to and thinking about divine reality.

Resources to Fight for Love

Religion comes from the Latin meaning "to tie together". It is intended to be a shared system of thought and action that offers a comprehensive view of existence for all to partake in. The different churches should be like instruments in a divine symphony, all playing together in harmony. All striving to advance the cause of love in the world.

> *"As the branch cannot bear fruit of itself, unless it*
> *abides in the Vine, so neither can you, unless you*

abide in me. I am the vine, You are the branches.
He that abides in me and I in him, the Same bears
much fruit; for without me you can do nothing."
(John 15: 4,5)

If the individual religious groups viewed themselves as branches of the same vine, we all would have abundant life (fruit). Because the life of the vine is love from God. If all the vines were connected, the life (love) of the vine could reach much further.

To say your little church is the only one favored by God is like claiming that the sun only shines on you. In John 17:21 Jesus prayed "that they all may be one, Father, just as you are in me and I am in you. May they also be in us so that the world may believe that you have sent me." If the Father is pure love and he is in Jesus, then Jesus is the personification of the Father on earth. He asked that we all be one or that we all share the love of God. How do we do that if we are so splintered off into so many churches?

Aren't we supposed to love everyone not just the ones who agree with us? Look around and you will see Christians hating Heathens, Muslims hating Infidels and Jews hating Gentiles. People committed to another faith are ridiculed and told that they are going to Hell. Loving people, but not saved, are going straight to Hell. All pitiful losers; lost and unsaved. If you share my beliefs, you are wise and spiritual but if you don't you are wicked and evil. Are we loving God with all our hearts, minds, souls and strength when we act this way?

Another way that God said we could show our love is by feeding the hungry, giving drink to the thirsty, clothing the naked, providing shelter to the homeless, healing the sick and visiting the imprisoned. These are acts of love. Maybe if some of the 100,000 churches joined forces to do this it would be a start toward reconciliation and a huge blow to entropy.

Religious groups should be love's best training ground for the "soldiers" in the war. It should be the place where people go to be taught how to improve their own love of God, neighbor and self; the place where we learn to identify entropy and its sneaky ways and how to employ love to counter it. Entropy snuck into our churches

81

and is causing a great deal of destruction through endless splintering of church groups, denominations, and faiths. Let's come together in love to drive it out of our churches and our lives.

Expressing "religious devotion" by hating, hurting or killing people of other faiths, is not God's will. God asks that we love one another, because we cannot honestly love God if we do not love *all* his children. His children include all the people of faith and ones with no faith.

Pay attention to today's fifty percent decline in church involvement. Over 2.7 million members drop out every year. Many more say they are church goers but really are only going on a few church holidays. About 85 million Americans say they are Christians but only forty to fifty percent attend church regularly. America appears to be going the way of Europe where only about three percent regularly attend church. By 2020, American church attendance had expected to drop to around fifteen percent. Church leaders point to "cultural decay" and "changing values", both forms of entropy, as the reason why. They recognize the enemy's work but seem ill-equipped to fight back with love. Rather than condemning those who do not go to church, ask them why they no longer go. Maybe by learning their reasons, church leaders could redesign the way they "do church". Some leaders will wince at the thought of changing the way they "do church". They think their way is timeless and should never change. Only non-living things never change. If the church is "alive" it must continuously change, grow, adapt or it will wither away.

We say that church is "alive" but unchanging. This is a contradiction in terms. Everything that is alive must change over time to stay alive. The church is no exception. The church should be organic, adaptable and alive, or it will atrophy. That means to stay alive and vibrant, the church needs to bring in energy and information from outside itself: from other churches and individuals. It needs to hear them out, process what they have to say and keep the best ideas increasing the life of their own church. But many times, pride gets in the way with church goers saying that God is leading *their* church, so he can't be doing anything worthwhile in other churches or faiths. Wrong. Rather than pointing fingers of judgment at other church leaders, meet regularly with your members and discuss ways to love more.

The "why" of creation is unchanging but the universe has been evolving and changing for 13.7 billion years. It would be like taking a picture of a baby and saying that it is the same yesterday, today and tomorrow. This confuses the person's "being" state with his "becoming" state. The "Body of Christ" (the Church) changes over time because it is still "becoming". Even Jesus had to physically and mentally develop over time and didn't begin his ministry until he was 30 years old. The "Spirit of Christ" does not change because it is the church's "being" state. When the Pope makes an "infallible" claim, he is talking about the "being" questions not the "becoming" questions. He is discussing the *why* answers. The "why" of the church has to do with helping human beings emerge on the next level of existence in Heaven. This purpose doesn't change because it is the "*being*" state of the church. Then the church must focus on ways to "*become*" better and better at teaching and training its members in how to love. Fighting about whether Mary was a virgin, or if Jesus had a brother named James, and other such sideshows is misdirection. It takes the church away from its purpose. Religion should not divide us but help us to build relationships, peace and love.

As the apostle Paul said, church members who follow all the rules but don't love are fooling themselves. This is what the Pharisees did, and Jesus strongly rebuked them. Bragging that you have followed all the rules while judging others as inferior for not doing so is not what God wants. Despising and attacking all who do not believe as you do, looking down on them and judging them has nothing to do with God's love and therefore should not be part of any religion.

One reason church attendance has dropped off is all those who defiantly declare that they have a personal relationship with God or they are "spiritual" and do not need "organized" religion. A "personal relationship" with God without being anchored to a specific church leaves you open to entropy's attack. It is like going into battle alone. Alone you will get confused by all the conflicting facts, misleading you because of your inadequate understanding of scripture or take control of that your inner voice that guides your thoughts leading you off track. How does that personal relationship help you learn to love yourself or others? Union with God, who is pure love, requires union with his family. That is why scriptures say, "whenever two or more gather" there I am with them. Love of God, self and neighbor are linked together as Jesus told the Pharisees when they asked him which commandments to follow. Relationship to God is not an individual thing just as love requires two or more to bond together.

Many who don't go to church have lost heart because of scandals about pedophilia or ministers who preach marriage fidelity and then get caught with a prostitute. Or they hear about other "men and women of God" who have stolen money or acted much differently than they preached proving themselves to be hypocrites: do as they say not as they do. Church leaders are human beings subject to the forces of entropy; they will make mistakes and even sin. They are doing God's work but still may fail. Remember it is God's church, not theirs. They are members, not owners of the church. Human failures should not be a reason to drop out of a church but to participate more. We are all vulnerable to the power of entropy and need love's reinforcement. When people of faith fail it is a reminder of just how helpless we all can be.

Most church goers don't even know the name of the person sitting next to them in the pew let alone the members of the church hierarchy. Unsatisfied parishioners of many large churches are leaving for small "non-denominational" churches (which really are denominations). Members of these smaller churches claim that they are better examples of what Christ and the Apostles wanted when they started the church. Church gatherings in the early church were small. Many were with just family members and relatives so, of course, people knew each other better. Small churches encourage personal relationships but splintering off into small groups makes the church more susceptible to attack. Many of these small churches are led by preachers that are not properly trained, rigid and dogmatic in their messages and judgmental of all who disagree with them. Some develop a superior attitude and believe that those who don't follow their exact religious interpretation of the Bible will go to Hell. Didn't Jesus say love your enemies, pray for your prosecutors and forgive those who hurt you and judgment is mine? Damning them to Hell, like they even have that power, doesn't sound like what he had in mind.

"As long as religions are competing for the keys to the kingdom of God, religion will cause as much harm as healing, division as unity, war as peace."
—If God is Love, pg. 13

Church needs to be a place where members share their lives, build loving relationships and learn how to love more completely and unconditionally. A place I can go to and be loved, accepted, healed, forgiven, restored and made whole when I'm hurting and where I can do the same for others. It should be like a hospital for the sick (the sinners) and a museum that tells its history and highlights its superstars (its saints and past leaders) but most of all it should be a place to celebrate, worship, thank God and care for ourselves and others.

The first third of our lives we prepare for the journey ahead. Because we have no prior experience to fall back on, people in positions of authority teach us all kinds of rules and regulations about how to do things the right way and avoid being injured. Then we step out on our own into the real world and, through experience, decide which of the rules and regulations apply to our lives and which do not. We prepare for life when we are young and then go out and live it as adults. This should be true of the church as well. God began working with His people by giving many rules and regulations. When civilization matured enough Jesus said, "you have heard it said, well I say this". He offered a more mature approach to life by his example and his love commandments. This did not make Jesus a "cafeteria Jew". It made him a mature Jew who understood the real meaning of his faith. This is true today, as well. Just because you don't blindly follow all the church's rules, regulations and doctrines, may not make us a "cafeteria church goer" but a mature one.

God showed us how to love through the life of Jesus. Jesus is the physical manifestation of God but limited by his human condition. A man who claimed what Jesus claimed—would be considered insane, Satan or God. He didn't spend his time writing down what was important. Instead he talked to as many as was physically possible (no internet or mass media back then) using parables and stories that the locals could understand, remember and repeat. He was a great teacher, leader, healer, miracle worker, prophet and much more. Jesus preached generosity, tolerance and universal love. He had very little money, no home and very few personal belongings. Yet he wound end up being the most important person who ever lived. In fact, our calendar is written "B.C.", Before Christ, and "A.D.", Anno Domini, in the year of our Lord. The birth, life, death and resurrection of Jesus Christ marked the most pivotal point in the history of the world. The politically correct crowd is working hard to change B.C. to B.C.E., before the common era and C.E., common era, to separate the calendar from reference to Jesus Christ. Changing the label still doesn't change the fact that the calendar is divided by before Christ and since.

Jesus taught that to do God's will we should feed the hungry, give drinks to the thirsty, clothe the naked, shelter the homeless, heal the sick and visit those in prison and he did all of those things. In other words, spend your time helping the people who are your real neighbors. These are our neighbors, not the person sitting next to us in church. We do love our fellow parishioners too because they are part of the church "body" along with us. When we love other members of the church, we are loving our self because we are all members of the one church body. But when we love those who are not part of our church, we are loving our neighbor as ourselves.

> *"Do more than belong: participate. Do more than care: help. Do more than believe: practice. Do more than be fair: be kind. Do more than forgive: forget. Do more than dream: work."*
> —William Arthur Ward

The major religions have done some things well. They have preserved the most important elements of their faith for thousands of years. They have preserved many historical documents and added current writings designed to explain their religion to the adult faithful. However, most church goers took religious education as children and stopped when they were still young teenagers. No wonder they have a childish understanding of their faith. People need reinforcement of what they believe throughout their adult lives. We need to be lifelong learners of what it means to love God, ourselves and our neighbors. Religion should clearly teach four primary things:

1. **P**urpose—The reason for living: to emerge in Heaven with God and those who love him
2. **A**ctions—The work needed to accomplish the purpose: love God and neighbor as self
3. **I**nformation—what is needed to know about love and how to measure our progress as we grow in love
4. **R**esources—The time, people, places and things needed to act

"PAIR" is what happens when we love, we bond with others. If churches would focus on how to love more, to "PAIR" up, we would all be able to come together with a common purpose. If the churches shared the worldview that, as Jesus said, the two commandments to love God, neighbor and self are the core convictions of the church, they would become the place we all go to learn more about love. Pick a church that puts God first, one that nurtures its members into becoming more loving people and then sends those people out into the world spreading that love.

In 1666, Isaac Newton, discovered that white light was, in fact, a mixture of all the other colors in the visible spectrum, from dark red to the deepest purple. The only way to create white light was to draw all these different colors together into a single beam. Jesus said he was the light of the world and since he is the son of pure love; love is the light that needs to bring people together. Religion needs to be a shared system of thought and action that offers a comprehensive view of existence for all the "colors" or types of worshippers. By joining together, the churches would be that wonderful beacon of light that points the world to God.

Other Training Centers of Love

At one time, schools and parents shared the responsibility of teaching morality, values and wisdom. That is until the 1960's when the Supreme Court outlawed school prayer and religious discussions in public schools. The unintended consequence of this action caused school age students to stop discussing purpose, morality and values all together. When parents complain about the violence, drugs, and the poor conditions in the schools today, they should thank the Supreme Court. Without the help of educators, churches and families need to work that much harder to instill the proper values in our youth.

Not everyone is interested in participating in a religious group or is part of an educational community. Over the years, civic, service and political organizations have attracted many people who wanted to be a part of something larger than themselves. They participated in a common cause and became friends. However, participation has declined sharply over the last four decades. Membership was highest in the 1950's and 1960's. From 1985 to 2010, Rotary dropped by a third and was projected to lose another third by 2015. The Jaycees had 140,000 members in 1993 and is down to 50,000 now, off sixty-four percent. The Freemasons are down 3.8 million members since the 1950's. The Elks are off 1.6 million since 1980. In the 1950's and 1960's most service clubs were exclusively run by men with local businesses and civic leaders who wanted to network and provide community service. They lived where they worked and wanted to make their communities better (love was winning). Adding women helped temporarily boast membership but the aging of members without adding new, younger people caused involvement to decline. Baby boomers who came of age around 1970 were not joiners. The Vietnam War and Watergate made them very skeptical of any organization. Generation Xer's and Millennials seem more interested in being self-employed and self-oriented (left alone or rather connected electronically instead of personally). A large majority of them rent instead of owning homes, because of astronomical educational bills or so they can switch jobs and locations every few years and use their money for personal gratification. They haven't been looking for leadership positions or personal interaction. They don't even like to talk on the phone, preferring to send text messages. They'll tell you it is faster because you don't have to waste a lot of time on "small talk". They manage their relationships electronically and feel social media gives them all the friendship and information they need.

> *"Americans are becoming less socially connected and experiencing more loneliness... People go to church less and less every year. We belong to fewer organizations than our predecessors did... Americans are less attached to society, their neighbors, their communities, other humans... Millions of Americans are alienated."*
> —Alienated Americans, P 92, 93

To turn things around, churches, civic and service clubs are going to have to change the way they operate. They need to encourage more face-to-face contact, interaction and conversation among their members. The younger adults who do participate want less information and more active involvement like building a house for Habitat for Humanity, serving the poor at food banks, playing cards or bingo. The leadership of these organizations need to show the members why their physical presence is important, breaking bread, sharing stories, having live action fun together (instead of electronic virtual fun).

Church, educational, civic leaders and politicians should form CEO Clubs like for-profit business leaders do. They can meet monthly to discuss the business side of their programs, but the emphasis should be on ways to get members to engage, form relationships and love one another. If these groups focus on what they have in common, many more people would want to belong to their organizations. They would look at the members and marvel saying, "see how they love one another" and "that place is where I go to find peace". We would all be on the same team, not working to undermine each other and letting those outsiders ridicule us for our inability to get along. Maybe we could even consolidate resources, sharing, cooperatively buying what we need, getting big quantity discounts and delivering results that are more cost effective. This would allow each group to deliver their message of love to a larger audience.

> *"In the world, in society, there is little peace because dialogue is missing...peace requires a persistent, patient, strong, intelligent dialogue... Dialogue fosters understanding, harmony, concord and peace."*
> —*Pope Francis*

Love Barriers

Even with a good understanding of love, we often find it difficult to overcome barriers of love. These barriers may arise from our experiences in the past: the hurts, wounds, rejections and disappointments that left us unable or unwilling to give or receive true love. The key to overcoming these obstacles can be summed up in one word: forgiveness. By asking those we have offended to forgive us—beginning with God—and then forgiving those who have offended us, we move beyond the cycle of bitterness and enter the realm of God's agape love.

"For a person will reap only what he sows, because the one who sows for his flesh will reap corruption (entropy) from the flesh, but the one who sows for the spirit will reap life (love) from the spirit." (Gal. 6.7-8). Life from the spirit of love, is more love. The prophet Ezekiel declared, "...the one who sins shall die" (Ez. 18.4), and the apostle Paul echoes, "For the wages of sin (entropy) is death, but the gift of God is eternal life (a life of pure love with God) in Christ Jesus our Lord." (Rom. 6.23). Said another way: give in to entropy and you will die but commit to true love and you will live forever. Reaping what you sow is justice in its purest form. God will show us the way, but it is up to us to take it. We are the ones putting the conditions on ourselves. If we turn our back on God, we let entropy overtake us. It is our choice to make.

Here God literally pleads with people to turn back from their self-destructive course of entropy and be saved by love. And in the New Testament it says, "The Lord...not wishing that any should perish but that all should come to repentance." (2 Pet. 3.9). (The Lord) "...who wills everyone to be saved and to come to knowledge of the truth." (1 Tim. 2.4). God wants us to make the right choice but will not stop us if we don't.

Our own self-centered desires—pride, envy and jealousy— often separate us from God's true love. This barrier can be overcome only through repentance, by turning away from entropy (sin) and asking God's forgiveness for our selfish desires and actions. As we humble ourselves before the Lord and receive His forgiveness, we will find freedom to look beyond our own needs and reach out to those around us. As Jesus said, "Who condemns you?" when nobody stepped forward, he said, "Then I don't condemn you either." Keep turning in the direction of His love. Do you need to ask the forgiveness of your neighbor too? Yes, this is where your minister or priest can serve as an intermediary between you and your neighbors. It helps to confess to another human being who accepts you unconditionally and doesn't judge you but forgives you.

Seek simple solutions to your problems. Remember that the more complicated you make them; the more likely entropy is at work. Love unites, creates greater oneness, harmony, peace, simplicity and life while entropy causes separation, disorder, destruction and death. Reconnect to other people, spend more time and attention on your family, become a member of clubs, bowling leagues, golf country clubs, and other social organizations. Most important, find a church that you feel comfortable with and get involved.

CHAPTER 5

———⊰※⊱———

Defeating Entropy

Guts to share my faith, guts to do the right thing,
Guts to live well, lead well and love well.
Guts to stand up in the face of challenges and hold
firm to God's promises.
—Brian Houston Live, Love, Lead p 195

The war is heating up. Entropy appears to be winning. We are becoming more and more isolated, alone and ineffective as a civilization. Religious groups are battling each other. Politicians are polarized on the far left or the far right. People would rather be alone with their electronic devices than spending time with other people. "Divide and conquer"; "a house divided against itself cannot stand"; "there is no I in team"; we have heard all the clichés. But they are true, and we need them today. If we don't turn things around soon and become more loving people, we are in serious trouble.

There is a popular Native American myth about two wolves that live inside each of us that are engaged in a vicious battle for control of our lives. One wolf, *the fearful wolf*, walks in anger, ego, envy, greed, resentment and lies. The other wolf, *the truthful wolf*, lives in appreciation, kindness, love, joy, compassion, and empathy. I would substitute the names of the wolves as, the *entropic wolf* and the *loving wolf.* When the myth ends, "Which wolf wins?" you ask, "The one you feed..."

The Good Old Days

I'm one of those guys that talks fondly about the good old days but, realistically, they weren't all good. We had a lot less to choose from, our medicine was not as good, information was a lot harder to find. There was segregation, neighborhoods that excluded people of different ethnic backgrounds, and voting by "party-lever". So not everything was "good" but there were some things that I remember fondly and wish they could make a comeback.

When I was young our television was black and white. Nights were spent together as a family watching comedy shows that told very funny jokes about all kinds of things, not just sex or politics. We had to choose between the three available networks. News reports in those days were considered unbiased (even though all of life is biased). Today, there are more than 50 free-to-air networks in the USA and another 200 plus cable and other types to watch. The major networks no longer hide their liberal or conservative bias. They pound away on political themes, pushing the liberal or conservative ideas and bashing anything or anyone who thinks differently. This leads to more entropy because there isn't a consensus about what is moral, or right, or just. Instead there are hundreds of splinter groups promoting their own point of view and bashing, labeling and separating all those who think differently.

We used to pick the channel we wanted to watch and then took turns jumping up to adjust the antennae to make the snow on the screen go away. We didn't have cable or fiber optics or remote controls. Pretty soon you'll probably be able to just think about changing channels and it will happen. I enjoyed time hanging out with my family, wrestling on the floor with my siblings and joking around. We developed our sense of humor by laughing together. Nowadays kids don't even sit in the same room with their parents or siblings. They stay in their own rooms, surfing social media (200 of the top websites have billions of users) or choosing from the hundreds of television stations and thousands of songs, videos, podcasts, and other options. How do they decide?

Television viewership is way down because there are so many other options available and because of all the commercials interruptions. A one-hour show has twenty minutes of commercials. Marketing people tell us that the two primary motivators to buy is happiness and fear. It seems like the emotion of choice is fear. Commercials attack our looks telling us we are too fat, skinny, bald, gray, blotchy, wrinkled and have flat chests and flabby butts. Americans spend billions on cosmetic procedures such as making breasts bigger or smaller, fixing noses and lifting eyes, injecting foreheads and lips with Botox, tucking tummies, doing liposuction and padding sagging rear ends. What are we doing to ourselves?

Television commercials attack our moods saying we are too grouchy, worried, jealous and are unprepared for college or retirement. We drive the wrong cars, live in the wrong places, and apparently do a bad job with personal hygiene and cleaning the house. They endorse miracle cures and spend, what seems to be forever, telling us all the ways that we might get sick and die unless and if we take their recommended medicine. There are vaccinations for almost every possible illness (some save lives but are we overdoing it with vaccines for everything you can think of). One commercial says it is very rare that our children might develop a certain illness, but we still should vaccinate them against it, so they don't die. The pharmaceutical industry is making us afraid to live by getting us to buy tons of ineffective drugs.

Every time we are given more and more choices,
we should consider that this is entropy at work.

Twenty-four hours a day someone is trying to sell us something. We are being told what it means to be successful and that we just don't measure up. Beautiful people tell us we are ugly, fat and lazy. They drive expensive cars and tell us we are losers for driving our average cars. We have developed so many "special" fields of knowledge that nobody seems to have general knowledge or common sense anymore. Fields that used to share information like science, religion and philosophy have formed specialties and gone their separate ways.

Nobody remembers that these "specialties" are really just different, narrow perspectives on the same reality. It has been said that the whole is greater than the sum of its parts but as more and more splinter groups form, will we ever be able to re-assemble the whole? If we can't, entropy gains more ground.

We are being overwhelmed by too many options or choices. Barbara Ann Kipfer wrote a book called *The Order of Things, How Everything in the World is Organized into Hierarchies, Structures and Pecking Orders.* In it she divided knowledge into thirteen essential areas: Earth Sciences, Life Sciences, Physical Sciences, Mathematics and Measurement, Technology, Religion, History, Social Sciences, Business and Economics, the Arts, Domestic Life, Sports and Recreation, and General Knowledge. Then each essential area was broken down into the ways they are further organized: hierarchies, structures, orders, classifications, branches, scales, divisions, successions, sequences and rankings. The book was published over twenty years ago, in 1997, so by now there are probably many more "essential areas" and ways to break them down that could be added to its 400 pages. No one person knows more than one percent of all there is to know. Because of this, people become specialists in their one small area of comprehension. Then they become so narrowly focused that they lose sight of the big picture. Life seemed so much simpler in the good old days.

Entropy wins by separating us and overwhelming us with choices that eat away at our precious time. When we are all in separate rooms with way too many choices about what to watch or listen to, we are missing out on time to love each other. We joke about all our available options but all they do is promote individualism and confusion. Love seeks to bring people, ideas and values together. Is it trying to direct you into the right way as opposed to many, many wrong ways? Yes, it wants people to share experiences, wisdom and lives. When we go our separate ways, entropy moves in causing disintegration, chaos and destruction.

We all should work to restore some objectivity to the airwaves. Media should be promoting ways to bring people together, sharing, not dividing lives. I'm not sure when it happened exactly, but somewhere along the way, news reporters turned into news commentators. They no longer report all the facts of a story, just the ones that support their opinion. This allows entropy to thrive. It can split us into many warring factions. It breaks up relationships, families and communities. And now with twenty-four-hour news stations, it bombards us all day long with divisive and depressing information that separates us even further. It appears to be more of a brainwashing technique than an information dispensing outlet.

We are told that the economy will soon crash so we better buy gold and survival food. We probably will die any day so, if we care about our families, we should buy tons of insurance. The more we listen to these ads, the more we lose our optimism, confidence and self-esteem as we cower in fear. We are told to make the best of today but keep getting bombarded with why tomorrow is going to be a disaster. Global warming became climate change when the planet wasn't warming. Now any change in climate allows some to beat up on the rest. Fear plays into entropy's hand making us afraid to take any positive action. It causes us to crawl back into our caves and hide from the rest of the world.

I shared a bedroom and a closet with two brothers and my four sisters shared two bedrooms. Today most kids have their own room. Again, not having to share with others. I got a new bicycle when I made my first communion and made others by cobbling together spare parts from old bikes. Today kids get a new bike every time they grow another inch. This teaches them wastefulness by casting away their bikes every year. People live in houses overflowing with plastic, indestructible, unused toys. So wasteful. Other than Wrangler jeans, I didn't know the name of any of my clothing "designers". Four-year-old children now insist on name branded clothes. We are teaching our children to be extreme materialists. They are not grateful for what they have. They are constantly comparing themselves to their friends and never seem satisfied.

When I was young, we didn't have "smart phones" we had ones with rotary dials (dumb phones?). We played board games like checkers, chess and monopoly or cards, not fancy, lifelike video games. The "old" games required other people to play but the video games can be played alone. The video game industry has revenues of over $115 billion a year. That means that way too many people are disconnecting themselves from others to play video games alone. Entropy always wants us to be alone, so it can do its evil work.

If it was daylight, we were outside playing with friends not alone texting them from the couch. Lack of exercise is making us lazy and overweight. Unstructured play time was a way to learn how to relax and have fun. It taught us how to get along with our peers. It gave our minds a rest and our bodies a workout. It reinforced our love for each other.

The streets were safe to walk, even at night. We would be outside, unsupervised, laughing, playing and having fun. Today, well meaning, over-indulgent, "helicopter parents" hover over their children making sure they are always safe and protected and never bored, idle or alone. They keep their children on rigid schedules of planned activities eating up all their "free time". They fill every available minute with organized sports, dance and music lessons, martial arts, art classes and one-on-one tutoring sessions. Children aren't making decisions about how to spend their time, instead they are passively moving as directed from one activity to the next. Their time must be carefully managed and not wasted. Time spent just having fun is considered inefficient and careless. As a result, we are raising a generation of young people who don't know how to schedule their own time, or relax, unwind, dream or just be. Failing to relax makes us uptight, over-stressed and susceptible to illness and disease.

Adults, with poor self-esteem, want to make sure their children have plenty of it, so they overwhelm them with praise. Now a young person that achieves more than the average kid is scorned instead of held up as an example of something our children should strive to be; and the average kid is praised. How many of you hate the New England Patriots and Tom Brady? Why is that? Schools are dropping the valedictorian and salutatorian designations at graduation because it makes those who do not win feel bad. Really? So, then we are raising a generation of *average* kids that are not striving to accomplish more or to be better people.

Besides "helicopter parents" there is another phenomenon emerging, "snowplow or lawn mower parents". These are the entitled parents that will pay anything to push their children along in life. They will remove all the obstacles in front of them so that they cannot fail. If they aren't good enough students to get into an elite college, they will pay off a coach or faculty member to move them to the head of the list. They have an abnormal fear of how their precious children will deal with any adversity in life. Some say they are more concerned about how others might view them as parents than how their children feel. Whatever the reason, they are robbing their children of some of the most valuable lessons they need to learn about how to handle hardships and disappointments in life.

We are raising a generation of children that are thin-skinned, self-absorbed, entitled victims. Everything we say winds up being a "trigger warning" making us a hater, bigot, or victimizer. When the wrong person wins an election, college students are given days off, or coloring books, bubbles, playdoh, pillows and blankets to help them deal with their painful disappointment. C.S. Lewis defined humility as "not thinking less of yourself" but rather as "thinking of yourself less." It seems like all the younger generation does is think about themselves. Anyone for a selfie?

> *"In the real world, people don't get paid to be selfish and disruptive, but, rather, to be productive members of society. They are rewarded for cooperation and teamwork, not for dividing people because they have negative feelings about another race or feel offended by those from a different socioeconomic background."*
> —Not A Day Care, page 15, 16

Homework is a lot easier today. Instead of doing research at the library or looking things up in books, kids use computer search engines to do their research. You can get an app for your cell phone that converts English into all kinds of foreign languages (oral or written). You can also get answers to math or science problems including the work that went into solving them. There are apps that take notes for you; right Alexa? The argument is, "If I can get the information from a computer why should I learn it?" Without knowledge, people won't know enough to think independently.

There are those who argue that today's homework is much more complex than in the old days. Yes, students can use their computer and calculator but that just means the homework questions can be more complex and thought provoking. This may be true if the student approaches his or her work honestly. The problem is that many will take the easy way out and Google the answers.

> *(In 1955) "Good breadwinner jobs for white-collar and blue-collar men allowed 80 percent of wives with young children to stay at home...nearly 90 percent of all adults were married by age thirty...almost all babies were born to married couples. 'Ninety percent of all first births occurred after the parents' marriage (about one in nine of those infants was conceived before marriage)...' 'Ever since the nation's founding', religious historian Phillip Hammond would note, 'a higher and higher proportion of Americans have affiliated with a church or synagogue right through the 1950's.'... Kiwanis Clubs, bowling leagues, American legion, labor unions, and local athletic associations were all booming."*
> —Alienated America, P 19,20

Everyone used to praise the intact family structure with a father and mother working together to raise their children. Today, most mothers work outside the home and too often are the head of the household. They spend all their free time chauffeuring the kids to their organized activities and complaining about being "stressed out". There were many large families in the old days, but today most married couples want no children or just one or two. They claim that they just don't have the time or money to raise a large family. Small or non-existent families helps entropy further separate us.

My mother stayed home to raise us, and my father was the bread winner. When he came home at five o'clock dinner was on the table. We all ate together and enjoyed talking about our day and what was happening in the world. After dinner my mother and father would have coffee and read the newspaper. They would describe key facts and highlights of stories they read. I sat there taking it all in. I learned a lot from those coffee chats. This mealtime ritual brought us closer together as a family and helped us understand more about the community and world that we lived in. It was a unifying event, increasing the love. Fast foods, microwaved dinners on the run, eating while watching television or taking food back to our rooms to eat alone are all ways that entropy infiltrates a loving ritual and destroys it. Today over 60 percent of families are dual income earners working long hours and traveling for business. No wonder we don't have time to do things together.

Parents used to take their nurturing and child development responsibilities very seriously. Today many seem willing to let the day cares and schools raise their children. John Dewey, an Atheist, is considered one of the most influential developers of public-school education. He claimed that teachers were the *true* prophets of the *true* God and were responsible for ushering in the *true* kingdom of God through proper education (or indoctrination). He was one of the developers of the Humanist Manifesto which stated that there is no God, no soul and no need for traditional religion. He was in favor of educational centralization to control the message of social transformation. Sounds more like a cult leader than an educator. The scary thing is, ninety-one percent of all school-aged children in this country will enroll in a tax payer-funded elementary and secondary school this year. These students will be drilled on the principles Dewey and others like him think all children should know. It is why home schooling is the fastest growing segment of American education at nearly two million students and rising. If we turn over the moral and ethical teaching of our children to these educators, how can we complain about them not seeing the world as we do. Our educational system is one of the leading causes of division in the world today. Parents prayed openly and passed their spiritual values along in the old days. Going to church was a weekly mandatory ritual. Today less than half the population go to church regularly. Even public schools used to allow prayer but not anymore. A recent survey said that two-thirds of all young people don't go to church. The sophisticated and educated liberal thinkers among us laugh at the notion of "sin". They label churchgoers as judgmental and prudish. To them, all people are good no matter what they choose to do or say. Labeling people as immoral is just evidence of the intolerance of those who believe in God.

We always had pets when we were young: dogs, cats, birds, rabbits and chicks at Easter one year. We loved our pets but never thought they were the same as people. Today many treat their pets as if they are people. Young couples handle their pets like we cared for our children. They send them to daycare, make sure they are groomed before holidays and worry about their feelings. They feed them gourmet foods, give them fancy places to live and seem content that their animals have satisfied their paternal instincts. These animals may be important to you, but they are not people. They are not the neighbors that God commanded us to love as we are to love our self. When we were kids, we went to see my uncle, our family doctor, for stitches, serious infections or broken arms. Today eighty-five to ninety percent of all doctor visits are for stress related illnesses; even children's doctor visits. Is life so much more stressful or are we over-emphasizing the things that stress us out? Chronic stress does lead to serious illnesses and diseases. No wonder the cost of healthcare is going through the roof. This super vigilant emphasis on ourselves: our physical appearance, our mental health and our insistence on always feeling perfect is helping entropy separate us further. If all I think about is me, I have no time to think about you.

In the good old days, we would go on vacation to a cottage on a lake and relax disconnected from the rest of the world. Today nobody goes on vacation without their smart phone, laptop, portable printer and whatever the latest technology is; basically, they bring their office on vacation with them. They never really disconnect and de-stress. Their car and their home are just extensions of the workplace. They don't take the time to just relax and have fun with family and friends. Watch how people sit at the beach and instead of enjoying the waves crashing against the rocks or a majestic sail boat catching the wind, they have their heads down texting away with music blasting into their ear buds. These people will be deaf in ten years from that ear pounding music and be nursing carpel tunnel syndrome from all that texting. Oh, and chiropractors will be dealing with a lot of neck and back problems from people always hunched over looking at their phones. I saw a recent news report that said young people are growing horns on the back of their heads (true story). They say it is from having their heads down so much looking at their phones. It sounds funny, but it isn't. This obsession with electronics is robbing us of seeing and appreciating the world around us and the people who want to enjoy our company.

The number of marriages is down by over twenty-five percent and people are waiting eight to ten years longer before getting married. Twenty-five percent of Millennials say they are unlikely to ever marry. A new term recently popped up called "Solo-gamy" which means marrying yourself (going solo). The individuals that are engaged to be married, are taking separate vacations before the wedding instead of going on a honeymoon after getting married. Some are not interested in getting married at all because they come from broken homes and are afraid that they will have the same thing happen to their family. Others admit that they don't want the "burden" of taking care of anyone but themselves.

> *(today) "Increased access to education, money, and career options for women and racial minorities meant increased autonomy. It meant they had more control over what they did with their lives. For women, that might or might not include marriage. With or without marriage, it might or might not include children. And with or without marriage or kids, life might or might not include a career and full-time job."*
> —Alienated America, P33

Marriage is part of God's plan. Children who come from families with their two biological parents see the best outcomes: less delinquency and out of wedlock pregnancies in adolescence, less school problems and better emotional health. Children born to unmarried parents are more than twice as likely to have no high school diploma by age twenty and less than half as likely to earn a decent income (AA, p73) Men who are married make a lot more money than men of the same age who are not married: about 19 percent more (Alienate Americans, page 75). Follow his plan and you will be better off.

Divorce was a word seldom used when I was young. It happened rarely, and nobody dared to talk about it. Today divorce and single parent homes are so common that nobody thinks about it enough to discuss it. Less than half the children in the United States live in traditional family homes. A third live with an unmarried parent. Married people who have children are called "breeders" and that is only one of the many available sexual labels and options. I cannot even keep track of all the other possibilities: homosexuals, lesbians, transgendered, bisexual, intersex, asexual, pansexual and Canada even has a category called "two spirits". One woman calls herself "masculine-of-center gender queer". I think the current count is seventy-six genders (entropy keeps separating us further). That doesn't even count those involved in bestiality, bondage, sadism, masochism, polygamy, incest and pedophilia. If we question anybody's gender or orientation, we are homophobes, bigots or misogynists and are interfering with their individual rights to choose their gender and sexual preferences. We can't say "he" or "she" we need to use pronouns like they, ze, zem, zir, or hir, zirs or hirs. This is a prime example of how language can cause entropy. Take two simple genders, male and female, and blow them up to seventy-six. Since when was choosing your sex an individual right? I have no problem with individuals choosing how they want to live their lives, just don't tell me how to live mine. Oh, and nobody needs to display their sexual preferences in public no matter what your gender identification is!

Let's return to the days when we said we were all Americans. Too many refer to themselves as hyphenated-Americans today. Identity politics is killing our unity as a country. It is pitting one group against another. Military leaders are concerned because they try to train American troops to work as one, cohesive unit. They say that identity politics is a cancer on the military. Today people want me to apologize for being a conservative, white male, senior citizen. I consider myself an American. My ancestors came from Ireland and Finland. I am grateful that they dared to cross the pond to America, but I was born here, not there. Entropy gains when people insist on hyphenating their identities.

During the civil rights movement, people marched to protest segregation and demanded equal rights and equal access to public places. They fought hard and won. Today the same groups want separate graduation ceremonies, separate lunch rooms, separate housing…separate, separate and more separate things. What started out with loving intentions has deteriorated into entropic separation. Immigrant sub-cultures don't want to assimilate, refusing to learn our language and values, and tearing our country apart (this went on in the old days too with ethnic neighborhoods, churches and schools). According to one count, there are over 350 languages spoken in US homes. Failing to assimilate leads to deteriorating inner cities and schools, high crime, gun violence and drug abuse and very poor communications. Many in these sub-cultures demand that the government support them through welfare, food stamps, school meals, and free education and healthcare. The US and state governments pay over one trillion dollars a year for welfare programs. Too many college graduates feel no need to repay their student loans. Others run up their bills and instead of figuring out how to pay them back, go bankrupt or lose their houses in foreclosure and blame it on the lenders or the government for not helping them. The government established a "safety net" for the poorest among us, not a free lunch for half the population. Money spent here is no longer available for the groups that are making a positive contribution to society.

In the good old days, families lived near their relatives and enjoyed spending time together. Now, with all the upward mobility, many families are spread out all over the country and hardly ever get together. People usually don't work where their family lives. A new term has popped up called "gig" economy. Many people prefer short term "gigs" or assignments rather than long term jobs. When the contract is up, so is the job. Gigs fit the modern mentality of not wanting any permanent commitments. With temporary employment, families do a lot more moving around. Entropy is infecting the workplace, separating people from their family, coworkers and friends.

Many of the jobs today involve telecommuting where people work from home. This keeps the corporate overhead down and may make commuting easier, but it also increases entropy. When people work together, they collaborate, innovate, share ideas and life stories and grow in love for one another. Talking on the phone or even through a video conference doesn't have the same effect. People are isolated, becoming more introverted, losing their sense of belonging and undermining the friendship and love that they have for each other. Without being connected, it is also a lot easier for management to lay people off. Employees don't care about the employer and can easily walk away from a job and the people from which they don't feel connected. Loyalty on both sides, the employer and employee, is disappearing. When the bond is broken, entropy increases.

Two hundred years ago, nobody commuted to work. People worked where they lived. Children grew up around their parents and other adults who taught them how to work and socialize. They gained wisdom, experience and communal skills with people of all ages. When people started working outside the homes, young and old went their separate ways. The young went to schools where they were divided up by age groups. They were only around people their own age and learned a lot less than when they were around people of all ages. This approach is contributing to the younger generation's lack of verbal communication skills and respect for their elders.

As children grow, they should learn to engage with others having different backgrounds, points of view, values and resources. Instead, many are afraid to talk to anyone (except through their computers using "BOTS"—stylized versions of themselves) because they have been warned over and over not to talk to strangers in person. Senior citizens have been pushed into nursing homes, senior housing or assisted living facilities and forgotten by the young. Seniors who were just around other seniors, tend to feel older than those who are around younger people. They feel like they no longer have anything worthwhile to say. They are fountains of knowledge and wisdom that we are ignoring. They are a source of love that could help unite us and, through entropy, are being shut off from all those younger people they could help.

Almost everyone you talk to is stressed out and approaching burnout. We are too busy with too many things to do, people to see, projects to finish, emails to read and appointments to keep. We have lost the ability to prioritize tasks and are constantly are running behind schedule, leaving work unfinished and feeling like we will never catch up. Yet many feel unfulfilled, unsatisfied and unappreciated. We are busy and bored at the same time and are living one-dimensional lives: working constantly. As the saying goes, "You can win the rat race and still be a rat". We have no energy, because we refuse to take time off for leisure, contemplation or appreciating life. Ambition is now a lifestyle. If we exercise or attend an out of work activity it is just to network or gain intel for the office. Ours has been labeled the "hustle workplace" with employees obsessed with striving, relentlessly positive, goal driven and devoid of any humor. Long hours do not improve productivity or creativity. You will not be lying on your death bed wishing you worked longer or harder.

Go to a restaurant and you'll find that most people aren't talking to each other, they are texting somebody else. It is like everybody is afraid that, if they don't keep in constant contact, they will miss the latest gossip or, worse still, somebody will be talking badly about them on Facebook, YouTube, or Instagram (each has one to two plus billion followers). The Internet has many advantages, but it also causes us to disengage from others in a real and meaningful way. Too many are perfectly content to manage their relationships via electronics with very little actual face-to-face time. They argue that the internet saves time, so they can spend more of it with family. But more than 40 percent of United States citizens use the internet. And since over eighty percent of communication is "non-verbal" just reading our cell phone messages is a totally ineffective way to communicate. Without good communication we cannot accomplish any meaningful purpose. We can't love others if we don't effectively communicate with them in person.

A high percentage of people don't even want to take the time to go to a restaurant, they prefer takeout food or drive-through windows. They would rather go to an ATM than a live bank teller or use the self-serve cash registers in stores or the self-serve gas pumps at gas stations; all ways to hurry up and avoid personal contact. More than two-thirds of Americans prefer self-service versus dealing with a company representative. Major department stores and malls are closing because too many people prefer shopping on-line. Doesn't anyone long for the good old days when store clerks cared about their customers and wanted to really get to know you? Many were your neighbors and it was one of the few times you saw them, so you looked forward to it. They knew what you liked and set things aside for you. Less and less personal contact with other people leads to societal disintegration.

Stores used to close on Sunday because people went to church in the morning and to family get togethers or long country rides in the afternoon. We did our shopping and chores on Saturday, so we could rest and spend meaningful time together on Sunday. Today stores are open on Sunday and many people work six days a week, so they shop and do their chores on Sunday. Church attendance has dropped by fifty to sixty percent in the USA and ninety-two percent in Europe. The excuse is that people claim to have a personal relationship with God and don't need to go to church to talk to Him. I wonder if there is a website for God. People don't feel the need to assemble with others to share in worshiping God and showing love for their neighbors.

When I was young, our house had a front porch where friends and family hung out and talked. People took walks and stopped by to say hello and catch up on what was happening. Today people prefer fenced in yards with back decks for privacy or they live in gated communities to avoid contact with others. Since they work most of the time and change jobs every couple of years, they don't feel the need to get to know their neighbors or get involved in the local community. There is a concept called "cocooning" where people are finding fewer reasons to leave their homes and interact in any way with all but a handful of close friends, relatives and associates. There are few gathering places left to go to like taverns, city parks, cafes or local stores.

The Elks, Rotary, Lions or Kiwanis were the places to go to socialize and to learn what was happening in your community. Now people just text or email each other for that information. Participation in these groups are way off and as Baby Boomers retire, there is serious doubt about how long they will survive. The cell phone crowd doesn't seem interested in bonding with others like we did in these organizations.

The things that people used to make by hand, they buy. Instead of fixing things, they just throw them away. Everything is disposable. Too many creature comforts are making us soft. We used to work hard and innovate because we were doing without and wanted something more, now we are getting fat and lazy because we have too much. Young people spend too much time living for today, chasing immediate pleasure through binge drinking and "casual hookups". They are losing hope of a better life, feeling confused and disengaged from everyone except the people on their cell phones and I-pads. When you are confused and disengaged, you are the perfect one to be scooped up into a cult or other splinter group. You can easily be manipulated into believing that all the traditional groups like family, church, communities are not what you want. And you are much more likely to commit suicide (a tread that is on the rise with young people).

Today over forty percent of adults' report feeling lonely and it is believed that the real number is much higher. This is also becoming a growing problem with young people as well. The young are turning to opioids and other drugs, violence, gangs, prostitution and suicide. Vice Admiral Vivek Murthy, the 19th Surgeon General, from 2014 to 2017 said, "During my years caring for patients, the most common pathology I saw was not heart disease or diabetes; it was loneliness." Loneliness causes weak social connections, disease, depression, anxiety, poor decision making, lack of creativity and more. Knowing how powerful the entropic power of loneliness can be should make us all want to improve our social connections, become more involved in the lives of our coworkers, family and friends. Instead kids are exploring hyperreality or virtual reality; that is pretend or artificial reality. It is better than the real world because you control the bad things that can happen to you. How does this prepare anyone for life in the real world?

All these modern-day, negative changes have occurred because of one thing, entropy. Entropy will destroy our civilization like it destroyed all of those that came before us unless we fight back. Entropy's statistics are staggering: for instance, there are 20 million drug addicts, 2.3 million in prison and another 3.7 million on probation and 17 million diagnosed with severe depression. Entropy is gaining on us and the only way to reverse the trend is to love more. We can increase the love by respecting police, military and other community leaders. We can work hard for our money, not just hope for the big pay day from government handouts, lotteries or law suits. Politicians need to go back to being statemen rather than spending all their time worrying about raising enough money to get reelected. They care more about their own self-interest and fund raising than legislating and compromising to help their constituents. We are a nation founded with the motto, "E Pluribus Unum", meaning "Out of many, one". This motto is the very definition of love. Remember, it is love that binds two together, bonds and unites us. If we don't start loving each other more, we will doom our civilization to being "E Unum Pluribus"—out of one, many.

So, when media throws too many options at us and ones that will negatively affect our values, morality and opinions what can we do? We can boycott the media outlet or choose which ones provide the kind of information we can trust, and that will help increase the love in the world. We can monitor and limit the time we and our children spent on electronic devices. Too much time on cell phones or computers or other electronic devices is destructive. Ideas like no device dinners are catching on. Families are reacquainting themselves with each other by forcing themselves to talk to the people in the room instead of the ones on the other end of their device. We should bring back the "family hour (or two)" where the whole family does something together (without their devices). Classrooms should collect the phones as students enter class and return them as they leave. Hopefully signal jamming equipment will become more available and schools can jam the signals to stop cell phone use during class time. When we go on vacation, we should leave our electronic office equipment behind and really disconnect and unwind. Instead of playing "group" games on laptop computers (with no exercise involved), go out and play a baseball, basketball or football game with friends. Play doubles tennis, pickleball or lacrosse or just hang out laughing and dreaming with friends in person. It is so important for human beings to interact "live" and not just on electronics. How about a live concert instead of ear phones? Give children space to fall or fail. Let them make some of their own decisions about how they spend their "free" time. Making mistakes, apologizing for accidents, overcoming obstacles are all a part of growing up. As G. Warren Nutter, an American economist, said, "Good judgment comes from experience and experience comes from bad judgment." It is part of growing up and preparing for life outside of the nest.

Get involved in a church. Show your family and friends that you love God and your neighbors by being present to worship and share the life in the "body" of the church. Spend time educating yourself about your religious beliefs. If the last time you learned about God and the church was as a young teenager, don't you owe it to yourself to learn about it from an adult perspective? Fight the people who are trying to remove all references to God from the country. Separation of church and state is a ridiculous concept. It is like asking you to separate your soul from your body.

About half of all Americans complain about feeling lonely and isolated. Since many jobs are being done remotely from home, there is less time interacting at work. Set up more face-to-face meetings. Workplaces could schedule more group "face-to-face" time in meetings, conferences and social events to build up employee bonds. With neighbors texting each other instead of getting together, more neighbors are lonely. Spend less time on your computer and cell phone and more face-to-face time with neighbors. Tear down the fences and build a front porch on your house. Introduce yourself to your neighbors and find ways to spend quality time together. Watch how your health improves and your interest in life increases. You will be more productive at work and engaged. Management will notice a marked decrease in people quitting their jobs. Love will multiply as it should.

Find out what your children's schools are teaching them. If it is an unbalanced liberal or conservative curriculum fight to have it changed. Children are supposed to be exposed to a balanced look at all kinds of world views. Narrow indoctrinations into one philosophy or another is not good. Let them get into healthy, well thought out debates about the pros and cons of different positions. Teach them to discern the truth by hearing all sides and deciding which is right.

> *"Classical education—truly liberating educa-tion—is about the common cause of personal righ-teousness, not the divisiveness of personal rights. Selflessness rather than Self. The unum rather than the pluribus."*
> —Not a Day Care page 192

Don't leave the raising of your children to others. Set clear boundaries, based on principles of discipline and punishment, that make it easy for your children to understand what you expect. Explain why your rules and boundaries are important for them to learn. Show them that e-mails, blogs, cell phones and computers block real human interaction and they need to limit their use. Let them know how much you love them and want what is truly best for them.

It can be a scary world, but we can't hide under rocks, lock ourselves in our rooms and stop interacting with others. Many are so afraid of being inconvenienced, hurt or suffering that they avoid all human relationships. When you were young, your parents told you, "Don't talk to strangers; they may hurt or kill you." The truth is much less than one percent of the children in the US get abducted and only one-fourth of them are from strangers. Three-fourths are from family members or acquaintances. One is too many but being obsessed with the possibility of it happening is an overreaction. Too many people are panicked about talking to strangers, so they grow up refusing to talk to or even be courteous to anyone they don't know. You can talk to strangers. You can ask an old man about his life when you ride next to him on a bus. Some parents teach their children to turn away if a stranger says hello. You don't want to get in his car but if you are an adult with your child, you certainly can be courteous. Take the lead and talk to a stranger and show your child how it is done. Children need to learn how to talk to adults in a kind and respectful way and you can show them how.

Let's reverse the trend of more and more specialization of knowledge and skills. We should not be specializing in any individual field of endeavor until we know enough about the broader overview of that field. And not all people should be specialists. We need generalists that can see the big picture and how it will affect each of the specialties below. We need people who understand the interconnectedness of all aspects of our existence. There was a time when the word "university" stood for "unity". It was a place people would go and learn how to integrate their knowledge of life, not segregate it into smaller and smaller compartments. We need to get back to that.

Think hard about what you need and what you want. You don't need everything you think you need. Don't waste time trying to keep up with the Jones. Measure your success against your previous best, not what Jones did. Making the best of now, doesn't mean wasting time carousing, overindulging or engaging in wasteful spending. It means knowing that "now" is the only real time you have, and you need to spend it doing what you can to love God, and your neighbor as yourself. Strive to be a "homo-aman", a loving being rather than just a "homo-sapien", a knowing being.

CHAPTER 6

⌒◉⌒

What Happens Next?

We know that we were born, live on average about 80 to 85 years and then we die. What we don't know for sure is what happens next. Some say that God created the universe from Heaven or eternity and that we will go there when we die. Others say the universe is all there is, and we just return to dust when we die. What do you think?

To forecast what happens next, we need to recap what we have discovered so far. Scientists tell us that about fourteen billion years ago, there was nothing: no time, space, energy, matter, structures, laws, or activity of any kind. There was absolute nothingness. Then, somehow, a tiny seed, smaller than a golf ball, just appeared with a temperature of trillions of degrees weighing trillions of pounds. It grew to the size of a grapefruit and with a thunderous thermodynamic force, it exploded in all directions, then, as the temperature dropped, the magnificent universe we see before us today formed. And it has been rapidly expanding ever since. It will continue to expand as the energy disburses and is turned into useless heat.

The minuscule seed contained all that was needed for the universe to emerge. Amazing (or should I say miraculous) that such a little thing could create the huge, wonderful, spacious universe we experience today. It is like the tiny acorn that becomes the mighty oak tree. That little golf ball sized seed, bonded together by God with His love, the first primal force. Then, the second force, entropy, tore it apart with a big bang spewing its contents equally in all directions. This marked the beginning of the real war to end all wars: the war between love and entropy.

More than half of all scientists believe that this universe is all there is which means they believe that something can be created out of nothing. The seed that started the universe, according to them, popped into existence from nothingness with nobody's help. Nothing caused it to exist. What was its purpose for popping into reality? If you wanted to build a house you would know why you wanted the house, the location where it would be built, the blueprints for the house layout, then you would locate the craftsmen and the materials needed to build the house. After all this pre-construction preparation you would start building. All these steps (causes) would take place before the actual construction (effect) began. But, these scientists say, our wonderful universe was constructed randomly with no prior preparation or planning. The materials appeared out of nowhere and were assembled without the skilled craftmanship of anyone or anything.

Scientists tell us for every *effect*, there is an outside agent that *causes* it. Everything in the universe comes from something else that already existed. That is, they say, everything but the initial seed which apparently had no cause and just popped into existence on its own and randomly created the universe with no construction plan or purpose. However, no other random universal seeds have appeared since.

Don't ask a scientist why this happened though, because science doesn't answer *why* questions. Scientists will tell you what something is, how much it weighs, what is its temperature and predict what it might happen next but not *why* it will happen. For answers to why questions, you need to turn to Ontology, the study of the guiding principles, insights and truths about why things are the way they are. Ontology involves mental concepts, so it means different things to different minds. Its answers are more difficult to quantify, it is messy but necessary because there are many things that science cannot explain or prove. It can't prove that rape is evil, or murder is wrong.

When people claim that science is the only way to know truth, it cannot prove that this statement is true. Science cannot prove that a one-time event happened in the past because it cannot develop a test to repeat the event to prove it happened. It cannot prove that your children or anyone else love's you. It does what it does well, but it cannot be our only way of understanding reality and truth.

Some scientists argue that the universe began with a flicker that happened once and never again. It was purely random but never happened again in fourteen billion years? Or that our universe may be one of many in a multi-verse and the seed was dropped here from some other universe. Then how did the multi-verse develop from nothing? Science cannot study absolute nothingness so it must create some "plausible" explanation instead of accepting the obvious, supernatural answer: God created it.

The physical processes and events that happen on a consistent basis and the regularities that follow laws of nature that we can know and predict accurately could not have originated solely and arbitrarily from the matter and the energy of the early universal seed. This universe which operates according to the same laws, forces and mathematical preciseness throughout, is supposed to have randomly emerged from the chaotic exploding of that tiny seed. A seed, they say, that was made up solely of super-hot sub-atomic particles and energy. How could anyone believe that nothingness could produce life, consciousness, awareness and love without the assistance of someone or something outside of the created universe? Can we all just accept the fact that God did it?

Rather than continuing to speculate, let's take a stand. There had to be some initial outside cause, that planted the "seed" (the effect). Absolutely nothing in this universe can produce something from nothing: it never has, and it never will. The universal first seed did not just randomly appear, then explode with a big bang creating chaos, spreading the contents of the seed off in every direction. It did not, arbitrarily, cause particles to join forming the galaxies, solar systems, planets and other complex structures. This scientific explanation is totally irrational. Before anything takes place, there must be intention to do it, a template that describes how it will be done and materials to build it. Therefore, there must be a designer outside of what is being built.

The material universe is like computer hardware that needs software to make it go. The universal software is the intelligence (or information) that had to be planned, in advance, and built into it from the beginning allowing the eventual emergent creation of all things.

The energy, matter, information, forces and laws that direct the universal expansion came from God. The rules of the universe are God's rules. Scientists believe that ninety-eight percent of all the matter that exists today was created at the time of the Big Bang, but that matter consisted of only the light gases: helium, hydrogen and lithium. None of the heavy elements like carbon, nitrogen and oxygen were present at the beginning of time. To create these elements, you would need the heat and explosive energy of another Big Bang but, as far as we know, there was only one Big Bang. These heavy elements are needed to create life so, where did they come from? How did they emerge from lower levels of existence? God did it.

The ingredients needed to make and govern the universe were not all cooked into that initial seed. The stars, galaxies, solar systems, planets and all other smaller universal structures were formed from the cooling of the tremendously hot energy. However, energy by itself could not direct all the expansion that took place. There had to be information supplied in that initial seed that directed the expansion and the forming of all the universal structures as the temperature dropped. Did that information arbitrarily assemble itself? No, of course it didn't. God put it there. Scientists can tell us approximately when the universe was "born"; 13.7 billion years ago, and they can see back to $10-13^{th}$ seconds after the seed first appeared. They see when the Big Bang occurred and how dense gas filled space as radiation, particles and energy waves disbursing evenly in all directions. They know that it has a limited but expanding border that is located about 90 billion trillion miles away from Earth. They describe the expanding universe like a balloon that is being blown up. So, the area of volume of the universe is increasing but there is an outer border or limit to it. If there is a border, a line separating two geographical areas, what is on the other side of the universal border? There must be some "geography" on the other side of the border or it wouldn't be a border. That is where the universe ends, and eternity or Heaven begins.

Scientists estimate that if the life of the universe were equivalent to that of a person, it would be a twenty-five-year-old. That is interesting because twenty-five is the age that most agree is when a human being is at his or her physical peak and the mind is fully developed. Maybe the universe is at its physical peak now. They can predict how long the universe will "live" and when it will "die". The universe is not infinite or eternal. It, like us, has a physical life span and will cease to exist. Science and western religion agree that the universe is not eternal or unlimited and if it is not, then no part of it, even its alleged consciousness, can be God. So, let's stop worshipping it and worship its real creator.

I have faith that the particles and energy fields, chemicals and gases, cells and systems of cells and the planets, stars and galaxies were not randomly generated from nothing. They follow the same instructions at the same time everywhere they appear in the vast universe because God created them to do so. Everything originated from God's plan which included the chaotic circumstances of the Big Bang and eventual unification of colors, smells and natural beauty. God created the codes and blueprints for every living and non-living entity. That is how the information came before the matter. God is the way that it began and became so organized from nothing.

God designed the plan or template so that the stars would release their stardust and direct it towards Earth. He made sure that the stardust included essential chemical ingredients needed to form living beings on Earth. God's plan made positively charged nuclei and negatively charged electrons develop into neural atoms. This allowed single-celled living organisms like bacteria to become nucleated cells which would eventually emerge as human beings.

The universe is not all there is. God created it in all its complexity but it is a miniscule part of all eternity. He wrote the instructions and designed the DNA that fashions every living thing. He gave purpose to every wave and particle. To Him billions and trillions are like zeros and ones. He knows every single one of us by name and loves each of us. He is much bigger and wiser than any human being and any human being that would deem himself God's equal is an arrogant, narcissistic fool.

> *"It would be very difficult to explain why the universe would have begun in just this way except as the act of a God who intended to create beings like us."*
> —Stephen Hawking

Maybe this universe is one of trillions of universes with other beings that God loves, who knows. All I know is that I have one life to live in this body and this universe has one, limited life too. I have this one lifetime to love enough to emerge in Heaven so I'm going to make the best of it. I'm not going to waste my life wondering if I will have a do-over in my next incarnation or if this one life on Earth is all I get. I am going to assume this is all I get. And I'm going to spend my life trying to love enough to emerge in Heaven. I'm not going to let entropy rule my life. I'm not going to be suckered in by entropy's misdirection and confusion. I won't let electronics or fear rule my life. Join me in fighting the forces of entropy with more and more love.

God wants to be one with us in Heaven for all eternity. This oneness is a unity in which God and each human being remains who they are and yet become part of a "composite oneness'. The Hebrew word for this oneness is "echad". It means a compound, multipart oneness as in a marriage not an undifferentiated oneness like the ocean. As Paul said: "But whoever is joined to the Lord becomes one (echad) spirit with him" (*1 Cor* 6:17). Our love must be channeled to achieve the desired result. Love, through emergence, takes two and makes them one without taking away anything from each but making the new entity much more than each was alone (we will not make God greater by a composite oneness with Him, but we will be much greater by joining Him).

So, we need to fill ourselves with enough love to, like Christ, explode out of our earthly bodies and emerge as higher beings in

Heaven. How do we acquire enough love to emerge in Heaven? We need to act out of genuine love, striving for unconditional love. Good intentions are not enough and even words of love are inadequate; what counts are actions. Although we can rely on God's promise to give us the hearts and minds necessary to love, we are weak and vulnerable. While on earth, under the influence of entropy, we are more than capable of acting against our better judgment. So, besides expressing love with our actions, we also need to ask God for the grace to carry out what we desire.

Humans are fragile and weak. We need God's supernatural vitamins to fight off the disease of entropy. Its power and forces are too great for us to fight without an injection of grace. We can live beyond our circumstances, problems, troubles and weaknesses if we ask God to strengthen us.

> *"Quit living as if the purpose of life is to arrive safely at death. Set God sized goals. Pursue God-ordained passions. Go after a dream that is destined to fail if not for divine intervention. Keep asking questions. Keep making mistakes. Keep seeking God. Stop pointing out problems and become part of the solution. Stop playing it safe and start taking risks. Expand your horizons. Accumulate experiences. Enjoy the journey. Find every excuse you can to celebrate everything you can. Live like today is the first day of the rest of your life. Don't let what's wrong with you keep you from worshipping what is right with God. Burn sinful bridges. Blaze new trails. don't let fear dictate your decisions. Take a flying leap of faith. QUIT HOLDING OUT. Quit holding back. Go all in with God. Go all out for God."*
> —"All In" by Mark Batterson

Love enough to emerge in Heaven and be one with God and all those who chose to love him and their neighbors as they loved themselves. It doesn't get better than that.

BIBLIOGRAPHY

Michael Anton, "After The Flight 93 Election", (New York: Encounter Books, 2019).

David Aikman, "A Man of Faith", (Tennessee: W Publishing Group, a Division of Thomas Nelson, Inc., 2004)

Fritjof Capra, "The Web of Life", (New York: Anchor Books, 1996).

Ernesto Cardenal, "Love A Glimpse of Eternity", (Massachusetts: Paraclete Press, 2006).

Steve Clark, "Growing in Faith" (Michigan: Servant Books, 1972).

Jim Collins, "Good to Great", (New York: HarperCollins Publishers, 2001).

Anthony Flew, "There is a God", (New York: HarperCollins, 2008).

Michael Fonseca, "Loving In The Master's Footsteps", (Indiana, Ava Maria Press, 2003).

Laura M. George, J.D., "The Love: of The Spiritual Paradigm", (Virginia: The Oracle Institute Press, LLC, 2010).

Kathie Lee Gifford, "The Rock, the Rock and the Rabbi", (New York, Thomas Nelson/ W. Publishing Group, 2018).

Bob Goff, "Everybody Always", (Tennessee, Nelson Books, 2018).

Joseph Green, D.D., "Pilgrim's Guide Cursillos in Christianity", (Texas: National Ultreya Publications, 1976).

Michael Green, "Jesus", (Oregon: Multnomah Publishers, 1999),

Pastor William R. Grimbol, "The Complete Idiot's Guide to the Life of Christ', (New York: Alpha Books, 2001).

Sean Hannity, "Deliver Us from Evil", (New York: Harper, 2004).

Bernard Haring, C.SS.R., "The Christ God with Us", (Montana: Liguori, 1999).

Michael H. Hart, "The 100 A Ranking of the Most Influential Persons in History", (New York: Galahad Books, 1978).

Christopher Hitchens, "God is Not Great", (New York: Hachette Book Group USA, 2007).

Mahlon Hoagland & Bert Dodson, "The Way Life Works", (New York: Times Books/Random House, 1995).

Robert R. Iatesta, "Fathers", (Michigan: Servant Books, 1980).

Stanley L. Jaki, "And on This Rock", (Indiana: Ave Maria Press, 1978).

Russell Re Manning, editor, "30-Second Religion", (New York: Metro Books, 2011).

Malachi Martin, "The Decline and Fall of the Roman Church", (New York: bantam Books, 1981).

Ralph Martin, "A Crisis of Truth", (Michigan: Servant Books, 1982).

Alfred McBride, O. Praem, "Essentials of the Faith", (Indiana: Our Sunday Visitor, Inc., 1994).

Kevin W. McCarthy, "The On Purpose Person", (Colorado: Pinon Press/Navpress Publishing Group, 1992).

Robert A. Muller, "Now", (New York, W.W. Norton & Co., 2016).

Arieh Ben-Naim, "Information, Entropy, Life and the Universe", (New Jersey: World Scientific Publishing Co. Pte. Ltd., 2015).

Mary C. Neal, MD, "To Heaven and Back", (Colorado: Waterbrook Press, 2001).

James C. Neely, MD, "Gender, The Myth of Equality", (New York: Simon & Schuster, 1981).

Adrian David Nelson, "Origins of Consciousness", (Nottingham, England, Metarisng Books, 2015).

Jeffrey Olsen, "Knowing", (Arizona, Envoy Publishing, 2018).

Madeline Pecora Nugent, Julian Stead, O.S.B., "Love-Ability", (New York: New City Press, 2007). (New York: HarperCollins Publishers, Inc., 2007).

Lisa Randall, "Dark Matter and the Dinosaurs" (New York: HarperCollins Publishers, 2015).

Michael Richards, "The Nature and Necessity of Christ's Church", (New York: Alba House, St. Paul Publications, 1983).

Derek Rydall, "Emergence", (New York: Simon & Schuster, 2015).

William Safire & Leonard Safir, "Words of Wisdom", (New York: Simon & Schuster, 1989).

Michael Savage, "God, Faith and Reason", (New York: Utopia Productions, Inc., 2017).

Robert H. Schuller, "Power Ideas for a Happy Family", (New Jersey: Spire Books/Fleming H. Revell Co.).

R. Edwin Sherman, "Bible Code Bombshell", (Arizona: New Leaf Press, 2005).

David J. Schwartz, PhD, "The Magic of Thinking Big" (New York, Simon & Shuster, 1965).

Lee Strobel, "The Case for Grace", (Michigan: Zondervan, 2015).

David J. Schwartz, PhD, "The Magic of Thinking Big" (New York, Simon & Shuster, 1965).

Jill Bolte Taylor, PhD, "My Stroke of Insight", (New York, Plume Penguin Group, 2006).

The Teaching Company, "The Great Courses: Great World Religions: Christianity", (Virginia: The Teaching Company LP, 2003).

The Teaching Company, "The Great Courses: Great World Religions: Hinduism", (Virginia: The Teaching Company, 2003).

The Teaching 131 Company, "The Great Courses: Great World Religions: Buddhism", (Virginia: The Teaching Company, 2003).

Eckhart Tolle, "A New Earth", (New York: Penguin Books, 2005).

Libreria Editrice Vaticana, "Catechism of the Catholic Church", (New York: Catholic Book Publishing Co., 1994).

Ethan Walker III "The Mystic Christ", (Oklahoma: Devi Press, 2003).

Neale Donald Walsch, "Tomorrow's God", (New York: Atria Books, 2004).

Jonathan Waldman, "Rust", (New York, Simon & Schuster, 2015).

Margaret J. Wheatley, "Leadership and the New Science", (California: Berrett-Koehler Publishers, Inc., 1992).

Christopher West, "The Love That Satisfies", (Pennsylvania: Ascension Press, 2007).

K. D. Whitehead, "The Need for the Magisterium of the Church", (Illinois: Franciscan Herald Press, 1979).

Margaret J. Wheatley, "Leadership and the New Science", (California: Berrett-Koehler Publishers, Inc. 1992).

Ravi Zacharias, "The End of Reason", (Michigan: Zondervan, 2008).

Ravi Zacharias, "Light in the Shadow of Jihad", (Oregon: Multnomah Publishers, Inc, 2002).

www.ingramcontent.com/pod-product-compliance
Lightning Source LLC
Chambersburg PA
CBHW021647120626
46545CB00002B/745